Sri Guru Arjan Dev Jee

A Short Biography

Translated & Edited by

Kuljit Singh & Harjinder Singh

Copyright © Harjinder Singh 2018

All rights reserved.

No part of this publication may be reproduced, stored in an information storage and retrieval system, or transmitted in any form or by any means, electronic, mechanical, photocopying, recording or otherwise without written permission of Akaal Publishers.

First Published by Akaal Publishers in 2018

British Library Cataloguing in Publication Data

A catalogue record for this book is available from the British Library

ISBN 978-1-9996052-0-9

Front cover painting by Bhai Gian Singh Naqqash of Golden Temple, artwork reproduced with permission of www.art-heritage.com

Cover Design by Harvir Singh

For further information see our website: www.akaalpublishers.com

All rights reserved.

Dedicated to

Sri Guru Arjan Dev Jee

The first martyr of the Sikhs

Contents

	Preface	1-3
1.	Birth & Childhood	5-6
2.	Gurgaddi	7-9
3.	Ramdaspur	10
4.	Toxic atmosphere	11-14
5.	Santokhsar	15-16
6.	Daily timetable	17
7.	Bhai Kalyana	18-21
8.	King of Mandi visits Harmander Sahib	22-26
9.	Harmander Sahib & Amritsar Sarovar Seva	27-34
10.	Bhai Hema	35-36
11.	Khaara & Tarn Taran	37-38
12.	Congregation of Agra	39-41
13.	Kartarpur of Doaba	41-43
14.	Birth of Sri Guru Hargobind	43-47
15.	Baba Mohan Jee & Gurbani	49-54
16.	Meeting Baba Dattu Jee	55
17.	Compiling Sri Aadh Granth	56-63
18.	Engagement Sri Hargobind	64-65
19.	Sulhi Khan	66-67
20.	Humility 7 Peshawar Congregation	68
21.	Plotting of Prithi Chand & Chandhu	69-71
22.	Sulbhi Khan	72-75
23.	Prithi Chand leaves for Lahore	75-76

24. Jahangir invites Guru Jee	77-78
25. Baba Sri Chand	79-81
26. Meeting Khusro	81-82
27. Message from Jahangir	83-85
28. Gurgaddi of Sri Guru Hargobind	85-87
29. Last words of advice to Mata Ganga	87-88
30. Leaving for Lahore	89-90
31. Bhai Suddhu Jee	91-92
32. Bhai Arth Mal	93-94
33. Chandhu burns with envy	95-96
34. Wazir Khan the devout	97-98
35. Guru Jee arrives at Jahangir's court	99-101
36. Guru Jee taken to Chandhu's house	103
37. The torture begins	104-105
38. Tortured by being boiled alive	105-108
39. Chandu's devout Daughter-in-Law	108-110
40. Tortured with burning hot sand	111-113
41. Saints seek permission to intervene	114-115
42. Tortured on a hot metal plate	115-116
43. Fifth day of captivity	117-119
44. Martyrdom (Shaheedi)	119-122
Glossary	123-127
References	129-130

God is realised by the True Guru's Grace

Preface

Sri Guru Arjan Dev Jee (1563-1605 CE) was the fifth Sikh Guru, he consolidated the fledging Sikh faith and institutionalised it. He built the Harmander Sahib which is commonly known as the 'Golden Temple' in the middle of the sacred pool which is called 'Amritsar' – which translates to 'pool of immortality.' Only God's praises are sung at Harmander Sahib and it is revered as the most sacred Gurdwara for Sikhs. The Sikh Scripture was compiled by Sri Guru Arjan Dev Jee. In effect Sri Guru Arjan Dev Jee created the heartbeat of the Sikhs in compiling the scripture and constructing Harmander Sahib.

This short biography is based upon partially on a short biography on Sri Guru Arjan Dev Jee that Bhai Vir Singh penned called 'Jeewan Parsang Sahib Sri Guru Arjan Dev Jee' – I have translated parts of this book from the Punjabi into English in order to compile this book. The second major source is of 'Suraj Parkash' by the poet Bhai Santokh Singh, the historical account of the martyrdom of Sri Guru Arjan Dev Jee has been used from 'Suraj Parkash.' This was done by using the English discourse that has been done by Bhai Kuljit Singh (Leicester, UK) narrating the martyrdom of the Guru. Bhai Kuljit Singh used the Punjabi discourse of the martyrdom that has been narrated by Giani Harbhajan Singh Dudike which he then translated into English.

For both sources – I have not used the material in its entirety and have edited and included other information that I have personally learnt over the many years I have conducted research on Sikh History and from oral narrations in Gurdwaras. Any errors in translation and editing are my own.

The book is thus translated and edited by myself – Harjinder Singh and Bhai Kuljit Singh. I collated all the research and edited the typed audio discourse of the martyrdom of Sri Guru Arjan Dev Jee as narrated by Bhai Kuljit Singh. I translated other works as aforementioned and selected what to include in the final draft.

Any Gurbani which is quoted in this book is translated using a number of sources but I have tried to stay as close as I can to the 'Faridkoth Tika' which is the first ever print translation of Sri Guru Granth Sahib in antiquated Punjabi/Hindi. The translations in this book are in English, which can be a challenge, but my best efforts have been made to provide accurate translations. More adept Punjabi readers are advised to also find the Shabads in their original Gurmukhi and read that too.

A glossary of terms used throughout the book is available at page 123 to assist readers grasp Punjabi and terms used by Sikhs. I have written this book as a 'Sikh' first and foremost, so honorific terms have been used in this respect, which fall out of the parameters of normal use of the English language.

'God is realised by the True Guru's Grace' has been used throughout the book in the header as a 'manglacharan' which is an invocation to both God and Guru to bless each page of this book. The blessing sought as a writer by myself, is that the language is respectful, appropriate and profound. The invocation for the readers reading the book is that God and Guru inspire them to develop further spiritually.

Throughout the book quotations from Sri Guru Granth Sahib Jee have been used – the referencing of these is by a simple number in brackets which denotes the page from which the Shabad has been taken.

Thanks to Sarveen Kaur for typing up the English discourse of Bhai Kuljit Singh aforementioned. Manvir Kaur is also thanked for typing my translation notes of the manuscript of this book. Surinder Singh of Art Heritage Amritsar is thanked for granting permission to use artwork of his grandfather for the front cover. Harvir Singh of www.ironinks.com is thanked for the cover design. Baljinder Kaur of www.baljinderkaur.com is thanked for giving permission to use her artwork throughout the book.

The front cover design depicts Sri Guru Arjan Dev Jee seated and in front of them is their son Sri Guru Hargobind Sahib Jee. There is a Sikh behind the Guru waving the whisk.

I hope the readers find the book inspiring and I welcome feedback for future editions.

Harjinder Singh

May 2018

God is realised by the True Guru's Grace

God is realised by the True Guru's Grace

1. Birth & Childhood

Sri Guru Arjan Dev Jee was born on 15th April 1563 (CE) at what is now Chaubara Sahib Gurdwara at Goindval, Punjab. He was the youngest son of the fourth Sikh Guru, Sri Guru Ram Das Jee, his elder brothers were Prithi Chand and Mahadev. His mother was Bibi Bhani who was the daughter of the third Sikh Guru, Sri Guru Amar Das Jee (maternal grandfather). His paternal grandparents had died many years ago, before Sri Guru Ram Das Jee started to reside at Goindval.

He was in blessed surrounds from birth, in the regular company of Sri Guru Amar Das Jee and his father who was to become the fourth Guru – Sri Guru Ram Das Jee. His mother Bibi Bhani was very devout and is seen as an ideal Sikh woman, who served her father and Guru with much fervour.

A famous saying is stated by historians, in which Sri Guru Amar Das Jee had given a boon to the young Arjan Dev when he had said 'Doita Bani Ka Bohita' which means 'my grandson will make immense contributions to the Sikh Scripture.' Thus it was the fruition of this boon that led to Sri Guru Arjan Dev Jee being the most prolific writer of Gurbani (the words of the Gurus, Sikh Scripture) and became the Guru who collated all Gurbani of Sikh Guru's into one anthology which was then called Sri Aadh Granth (the first Granth/anthology).

Sri Guru Arjan Dev Jee is described by historians as an obedient son, who was always softly spoken. He was peaceful in outlook, humble and very intelligent. In Gurbani penned by Bhatt Kal he is described as being born with divine enlightenment in the following way:

He was revealed in the house of Sri Guru Raam Dass,

and all hopes and desires were fulfilled (the heir to the Guruship was born). From birth, He recognised God (had enlightenment) and the teachings of the Gurus. (1406)

The mission of Sri Guru Arjan Dev Jee is introduced here too by Bhatt Kal:

The Lord brought Him into the world, to practice the Yoga of devotional worship (Bhagti). Like Raja Janak the Guru was to live in the world like a king and be devoted to God – this was now to be the teaching for Sikhs to be householders and practice their faith. The word of the Guru's has been revealed (Sri Aadh Granth), and the Lord dwells on His tongue (in his writings of Gurbani). (1406)

2. Gurgaddi Sri Guru Arjan Dev Jee

Sri Guru Ram Dass Jee created the Sarovar (water tank) named 'Amritsar' which literally translates to 'pool of immortality.' This sarovar has healing and mystical properties due to the continuous recitals of Gurbani in its vicinity. In the middle of this 'Amritsar' Sri Guru Ram Dass Jee had created a platform where prayers were recited.

In September 1581 CE Sri Guru Ram Dass Jee visited Goindval and suddenly departed for their eternal abode – leaving their physical body. Before departing they had appointed Sri Guru Arjan Dev Jee as the next Guru. Bhatt Harbans has described this occurrence befittingly in Gurbani:

It was the Will of God that Sri Guru Ram Dass went to his heavenly abode (passed). He gave the throne of God (to Sri Guru Arjan Dev Jee) and seated the Guru upon it. The angels were delighted; they proclaimed and celebrated Your victory (of becoming the next Guru). The demons ran away; their sins made them shake and tremble inside (people like Prithi Chand). Those people who accepted Sri Guru Raam Dass Jee were blessed and their sins were abolished, He gave the Royal Canopy and Throne of the earth to Sri Guru Arjun, and came home. (1409)

Sri Guru Arjan Dev Jee went to Goindval and Sikhs and family members had flocked from far and wide to be present for the fourth Guru Jee's final rites. Prithi Chand the eldest son of Sri Guru Ram Dass Jee had also hastily made his way there. He was unhappy as he had not received the Guruship. He complained constantly to family members and Baba Budha Jee, (and other respected Sikhs), speaking harsh words in attempts to ensure he was given the 'Dastar' (turban) on the day of the final rites of his father.

When fathers die in Punjabi families, the tradition is for a turban to be tied on another male family member to signify that they are now the head of the family in place of the father.

The close family and friends wanted to give the 'Dastar' to Sri Guru Arjan Dev Jee in line with him receiving the Guruship from Sri Guru Ram Dass Jee. The day for the 'Dastar tying' ceremony dawned and relatives and Sikhs had congregated. Prithi Chand, Mahadev and Sri Guru Arjan Dev Jee were all present. This was not just a family programme but an event of Gurmat (imparting the teachings of the Guru's), family members were although in attendance to officiate the 'Dastar tying,' as is the familial tradition. First, Prithi Chand had left Goindval as he knew he had little support and following there. But after careful consideration he returned to Goindval and was now waiting for events to unfold, he was present with some of his supporters.

The greatness of Sri Guru Arjan Dev Jee was such that they were devoid of any feelings of enmity and Baba Mohri Jee (the son of Sri Guru Amar Das Jee) tied the 'Dastar' on Sri Guru Arjan Dev Jee. Sri Guru Arjan Dev Jee walked over to Prithi Chand and said in a loving melodic voice, *"Brother here have this turban, tie this upon your head. Let us be brothers and I will tie this turban upon your head."* Maharaj cooled the whole situation with their loving nature, by this act of humility. The congregation present praised Guru Jee and Sri Guru Ram Dass Jee for giving the Guruship to such a thoughtful and compassionate being. So, even here Sri Guru Arjan

Dev Jee did not allow the final rites of Sri Guru Ram Dass Jee get ruined with any ill-feeling, rather, they neutralised any chance of bitterness and won over everyone present. Guru Jee came to abolish the grief of humanity with their benevolence and started out with this act, many more were to follow.

3. Ramdaspur & Goindval

After the final rites of Sri Guru Ram Das Jee Prithi Chand went to 'Ramdaspur', which was then the name of what is now known as the city of Amrtisar. Sulhi Khan a Mughal government official was passing through the area with some soldiers and Prithi Chand met with him and showered him with gifts, to increase his friendship with him. He then went on to inform Sulhi Khan of his predicament, making false accusations that Sri Guru Arjan Dev Jee had taken the Guruship with force and that the 'Dastar' was actually tied upon himself. He appealed to Sulhi Khan to assist him in opposing Sri Guru Arjan Dev Jee. Sulhi Khan agreed to help him. Prithi Chand was very happy with this alliance. At Ramdaspur Prithi Chand had begun his attempts to declare himself as the next Guru of the Sikhs whilst also hatching plots to destabilise any power Sri Guru Arjan Dev Jee had.

Elsewhere, Sri Guru Arjan Dev Jee stayed on at Goindval Sahib for some months. After which Guru Jee thought the time to follow the commands of Sri Guru Ram Dass Jee had now come, to make the Sarovar a more permanent structure and to now construct Harmander Sahib in the middle of the Sarovar. The other instruction was to also continue the nation building of the Sikhs that the preceding Guru's had started. This was to be done with the construction of Harmander Sahib where prayers were to commence 24 hours a day.

Two distinct camps had developed. Sri Guru Arjan Dev Jee was spreading love and enlightenment, whereas Prithi Chand was imbuing a spirit of hatred, opposition and greed.

4. Toxic atmosphere at Ramdaspur

Sri Guru Arjan Dev Jee upon returning to Ramdaspur realised that Prithi Chand was attempting to jostle support and income from the land and buildings that Sri Guru Ram Dass Jee had purchased. Guru Sahib realised that they would have to appease both of their brothers to ensure there was no conflict. In order to do this, Maharaj the merciful, gave some rental income from shops and buildings sent directly to Prithi Chand and some to Mahadev. In doing this they tried to be amicable and share income from their father's capital, even though this was all actually income for the Sikh Guru and not necessarily a family right to claim this income.

The more appeasing Sri Guru Arjan Dev Jee became the more opposing Prithi Chand became. Prithi Chand employed some men who would gather the incoming congregation and take them to Prithi Chand and say he is the Guru. He also employed some Masands (preachers) who would go out and preach about him being the Guru, they would collect charitable donations towards him and send Sikhs masses to him.

The epitome of forgiveness Sri Guru Arjan Dev Jee just peacefully endured this ongoing enmity. They did not attempt to counter Prithi Chand and create more hostility. The provision of Lanagr (free food) by Sri Guru Arjan Dev Jee continued and all Sikhs and visitors partook in it. Prithi Chand would also bring his followers to daily eat in the Langar. He did this to increase the burden of expenditure upon the administration of Guru Jee. Guru Sahib had already forfeited much income meant for his administration to his brothers but now more pressure on even the existing income was also exerted by these actions.

The savings Guru Sahib had brought from Goindval had now all been spent. Now, Sri Guru Arjan Dev Jee sold jewellery owned by their mother and wife, continuing the provision of Langar with this money. Prithi Chand would take donations off Sikhs coming to Ramdaspur as the Sikhs would unknowingly trust him as a respected elder of the family of the Guru. Guru Sahib was immovable in their patience and forgiving nature and still did nothing in response. Historical sources state that the Langar became very simple in its menu and provision, due to financial pressures.

Bhai Gurdas Jee (1551-1636) was a devout and respected Sikh. He was the maternal uncle (Mama) of Sri Guru Arjan Dev Jee. He had been sent to Agra by Sri Guru Ram Dass Jee to preach there, he now made his way back to Ramdaspur. He was happy with Sri Guru Arjan Dev Jee becoming the next Guru and became a devout Sikh of theirs too.

As a respected elder he learnt of the actions of Prithi Chand and Mahadev, he discussed the matter with his sister Bibi Bhani Jee and they agreed it was best for him to first convince the two elder brothers that what they were doing was wrong. This ploy failed and only greed could be seen in the outlook of Guru Sahib's brothers.

Bhai Gurdas Jee could not tolerate the way in which the visiting congregations were being duped and mistreated. Devout Sikhs would visit with gifts and to get their desires fulfilled. Many would leave distraught after learning they had wrongfully submitted their gifts and donations to Prithi Chand and rather than leaving uplifted, they would leave deflated.

Bhai Gurdas Jee was overwhelmed by respect and adoration for Sri Guru Arjan Dev Jee who was singularly relying on the will of God in this predicament of administration of Ramdaspur. But, he was also pained to not be able to help the visiting congregations benefit more from their visits after the creation of the Sarovar of Amritsar. Bhai Gurdas Jee realised Guru Sahib had no desire for wealth accumulation and had just followed the steps of previous Gurus by not reacting in a hateful manner to Prithi Chand and Mahadev.

Bhai Gurdas Jee also knew that a solution needed to be developed. So he got the much respected Baba Buddha Jee to come back to Ramdaspur from their abode and he got other famous visiting preachers such as Bhai Salo, Bhai Jaitha, Bhai Paira and Guru Sahib's family members from Goindval such as Baba Mohri Jee to all come to Ramdaspur. They collectively decided that a dwelling would be set up at about 7.5km from Ramdaspur upon the main road and the truth about the administration of Ramdaspur would be told to incoming congregations. At this spot, now stands Gurdwara Pipli Sahib, Amritsar. Similarly, another building was set up in the opposite direction to also get to incoming Sikhs. Then, letters were sent far and wide to Sikh congregations, which were signed by Bhai Gurdas Jee, Baba Buddha Jee and other prominent Sikhs. These letters told the truth about the acts of Prithi Chand and ensured Sikhs knew that Sri Guru Ram Das Jee had appointed Sri Guru Arjan Dev Jee as the next Guru.

Due to the actions of these prominent Sikhs the truth about the situation of Ramdaspur spread throughout the Sikh world. Sikhs from far off locations now specifically started to travel in to congregate with Guru Sahib. Wealthy Sikhs sent large sums of money to ensure the Langar was running at full capacity and Prithi Chand's followers now failed in their attempts to dupe the Sikh masses – the truth prevailed.

Mahadev and Prithi Chand now feared losing the rental income from the shops and buildings that Guru Sahib had verbally approved and redirected to them. Fearing the loss of this income Guru Jee's elder brothers approached Bhai Gurdas Jee as their maternal uncle (Mama) to get this rental income formally approved in writing on a permanent basis. Bhai Gurdas Jee and Guru Jee agreed to draw up the necessary paperwork and duly signed over the rental income.

One further problem remained, only Prithi Chand had offspring, his son Mehrban. Sri Guru Arjan Dev Jee had no children, so in terms of inheritance, at this point – Mehrban was in line to inherit everything, if the situation did not change. So, Prithi Chand thought he could still usurp the power and wealth of the house of the Guru in the future with his son becoming the next Guru.

5. Santokhsar

At the Gurdwara Santokhsar, Amritsar, there is an ancient tree, Sri Guru Ram Dass Jee and Sri Guru Arjan Dev Jee used to sit under this tree and give sermons to their Sikhs. The excavation for a Sarovar had been started here by Sri Guru Ram Dass Jee, now Sri Guru Arjan Dev Jee got the excavation works restarted to complete the construction of the Sarovar.

A building was uncovered during the excavation works. A yogi was found inside the building he was seated in meditation, in a samadhi (trance of meditation) but he was not breathing. Some yogis and other spiritually adept individuals can meditate and take their breath into their tenth gateway of the body (Dasam Duar) – when done, the body stops physically breathing but maintains life. The Sikhs were told to massage the yogi, after which, he started breathing again and came out of his trance of meditation.

The yogi said he was a meditative who had asked for liberation from his Guru. His Guru had ordered him to build this building he had been in and to go into meditative pose while putting his breath in his tenth gate and to stay here until Sri Guru Arjan Dev Jee finds him. He said Guru Jee will then liberate him. Upon learning that he had finally met Sri Guru Arjan Dev Jee, the yogi fell at Guru Jee's feet and begged for liberation. Guru Jee granted his wish and soon after, he passed away.

A Sikh from Peshawar called Santokh donated 250 coins (money) to Guru Jee and asked for his name to become eternal in the world. Maharaj granted his wish, using his donation to complete this Sarovar and named it after this Sikh, 'Santokhsar,' which translates as the pool of Santokh (contentment). This Sarovar was completed in 1588 CE and the project to make the Amritsar sarovar a permanent structure was also started in this year.

6. Daily timetable

Guru Jee would wake up at approximately 2am, they would then bathe. After which they would sit in meditation of God becoming fixated and imbued. The Rababis (rebeck players) would then arrive and start to sing Asa Dee Vaar (a morning hymn about how to conduct one self). The congregation would attend this service, both locals and visiting Sikhs. Everyone would become detached from worldly affairs when listening to the spiritually uplifting Kirtan and enjoy the electrifying aura. Guru Jee would then come and sit in the open at the end of the Kirtan – answering questions and listening to the desires of their Sikhs. Guru Jee would attend to each Sikh with love, dispelling doubts and imparting wisdom. Many times it would get as late as 8am by the time this had finished.

Sometime before 11am – breakfast would be served in the Langar. Guru Jee along with the congregation would then partake in this meal. After everyone had eaten to their content, Maharaj would leave to take rest. After 2pm a service would be held again and Guru Jee would deliver a discourse (Katha) to inspire and enlighten those congregated. Then just before sunset a service would be held in which Kirtan would be sung and the evening prayer (Rehras) would be read, after which everyone would eat their evening meal in the Langar. The night prayer before sleeping of 'Kirtan Sohila' would sometimes be listened to by Guru Jee at home or in the evening service with the congregation.

7. Bhai Kalyana

The construction of Harmander Sahib (temple of God, which is in the middle of the Amritsar sarovar) had now commenced. Orders of the Guru (Hukamnamme) were sent across the Sikh world to inform Sikhs of the construction project – so Sikhs could donate towards it and also volunteer to help.

Bricks and mortar were needed in large quantities to build Harmander Sahib and make the Amritsar Sarovar into a permanent structure. Prominent Sikhs went far and wide to spread the message of the construction works.

Baba Buddha Jee was appointed the lead for the construction, he supervised all the work. He sat under a tree which is now commonly referred to as 'Ber Buddha Jee' which is still on the bank of the Amritsar Sarovar. It was from here that the supervision took place. Bhai Gurdas Jee was in charge of all the paperwork and accounting of the construction.

Many Sikhs went off to far off places and different countries to fundraise for the construction. Bhai Kalyana went into mountainous regions and an area called 'Mandi' (today the Mandi City is in the Indian state of Himachal Pardesh). He stayed here finding it very scenic and started to do Kirtan here, people learnt of his saintly nature and started to congregate with him.

After a few days of being in Mandi it was 'Janam Ashtmi' the birthday of Krishan Bhagwan, the Hindu Prophet. The king of the locality said all the subjects in his kingdom are to fast at night, in the mornings they are to go to the temple and worship the idol there and break their fast after taking water which had been passed over the idol. Everyone obeyed this command apart from Bhai Kalyana. As Krishan Bhagwan was not his Guru Bhai Kalyana did not want to participate. The king learnt of this violation of his command, he called Bhai Kalyana to his court and asked why he had violated the command.

Bhai Kalyana: *"Oh King, you should not force your subjects to practice your faith, they should be free to practice what faith they like".*

King: *"Are you an atheist? Why are you asking for independence to practice your faith?"*

Bhai Kalyana: *"I am not an atheist. I pray to God."*

King: *"Then why do you refuse to do pooja (pray as prescribed by the King)?"*

Bhai Kalyana: *"I do not pray to an idol which is lifeless. I pray to God who is present everywhere, the illuminator of everything – I have faith in Him. God is not limited to being present in one idol."*

King: *"Imprison him! He is calling God a stone (the idol). He is an atheist and a 'Malech' (offensive term for a foreigner), although he looks like a Hindu."*

The next day Bhai Kalyana was brought to the King's Court and questioned again. He was ordered to bow to the idol or show where his all pervading God is now or wise Guru?

King: "Put your hands on your ears and bow and we will forgive you!"

Bhai Kalyana: "King, my Guru is Sri Guru Arjan Dev Jee, the current Guru in the lineage of Guru Nanak. My God is present at all places and times. His image is Immortal. I am a follower of my Gurus. I will not bow in front of the stone idol."

King: "Show me your Guru and invisible God! Take him away, break his leg and eject him from my kingdom, push him over the border into the next country."

Upon hearing this Bhai Kalyana closed his eyes, he concentrated upon the Guru, 'Support me, this is a matter of respect for the house of Guru Nanak – please protect me'. Bhai Kalyana became imbued in His prayer.

Whilst the king was fuming in anger, his lips started trembling, his face went red as fire, his whole head started to shake. He yelled *"Executioner, executioner"* and he fell unconscious. Commotion broke out whilst everyone started to attend to the King, using fans, applying wet towels and trying to bring the King around to consciousness again. A doctor that was there, checked his pulse, opened his mouth, splashed him with cold water wiped a wet towel upon his forehead but nothing worked. Then a wise person spoke and said, *"The King has been unjust in ordering such a harsh punishment for this visitor (Bhai Kalyana), just because he believes in God who is everywhere – how is this a punishable crime? Beg him for forgiveness, make him happy; take the executioner away (when saying 'executioner' the King had wanted to now execute Bhai Kalyana but had fallen unconscious when giving the order)."*

A minister did just this and asked Bhai Kalyana for forgiveness, Bhai Kalyana said, *"Bad actions are the enemy of a person, I pray to the God who has no enmity (meaning Bhai Kalyana still didn't wish ill of the King). Your King disrespected my Guru to whom I prayed to for assistance. If the King comes back to consciousness – you should all come with me, to meet my Guru and learn from them."* The minister said, *"Save the King's life. As you say will then happen."* Hearing this Bhai Kalyana asked for water, he then concentrated upon Sri Guru Arjan Dev Jee whom he could see before his eyes and he prayed in the following way, *"Oh Master, you are the form of Sri Guru Nanak Dev Jee, Sri Guru Arjan Dev Jee – bless the King, forgive his mistake, grant him consciousness. All these people now understand their mistake, they are now in your sanctuary, Oh destroyer of grief. Bless us."*

After saying this Bhai Kalyana splashed water over the eyes and face of the King. The King came around and was now back in his senses. He is still very weak but was now conscious. The King spoke in a very weak voice, *"Free the visitor, grant him honour and respect him."*

The King was taken for rest and after a few days of recovery he called Bhai Kalyana to meet him. He said, *"Your Guru is all powerful. Take me to him, so he can liberate me too."* Bhai Kalyana agreed to take the King to Maharaj.

8. King of Mandi visits Harmander Sahib

Bhai Kalyana set off with the King to get the blessed company of Sri Guru Arjan Dev Jee. They took with them the accompaniments of the King, servants, advisors, tents (for accommodation) and all they would need for the travel from Mandi to Ramdaspur.

One day after arriving at Ramdaspur, the King heard Guru Jee reading the prayer called 'Dakni Oankar' and heard the following lines being recited:

O Friend the inscription of destiny inscribed by the Creator Lord cannot be erased. God who created the universe, mercifully installs His Shabad within us (God's feet are the scripture). Glorious greatness rests in the hands of the Creator; reflect upon the Guru's Shabad to understand this. This inscription (of destiny) cannot be changed. As it pleases You, You sustain me God. By Your Glance of Grace, I have found peace; Nanak says reflect upon the Shabad. (937, Sri Guru Nanak Dev Jee)

The King bowed at the feet of Guru Jee and sat down. His mind raced in thoughts, after hearing these lines he thought, 'If what is written in our fate cannot be altered then what is the point of taking the sanctuary of Guru Jee?' He was embarrassed to ask at first but after getting courage he asked, *"Guru Jee, if we are to undergo our fate then what is the point of becoming a Sikh of the Guru? I have come with a specific desire to be fulfilled – how can that be achieved?"*

Guru Jee was enjoying the elixir of the recitation of Gurbani and did not want to speak much, but they said, *"Fate is not altered, but betterment can still be achieved. You undergo fate but obstacles are removed too: with the*

God is realised by the True Guru's Grace

mercy of the Guru happiness can be achieved." The King could not understand what was said and asked, *"How can both fate and the change of it occur?"* Guru Jee replied, *"King, if you stay a few days then you will learn what it means. But you will only understand it, when you undergo it, which will occur when you become Sri Guru Nanak Dev Jee's."*

Upon hearing this the King thought it is my misunderstanding and what Guru Jee says is correct. He fell at Guru Jee's feet, got Naam (God's name directly from the Guru as part of the initiation ceremony) and became a Sikh. He then went to rest. In the evening service he came and congregated, listening to Rehras Sahib. But the same question kept bugging him, 'how could one get blessed and still undergo their fate?' He ate his evening meal and went to sleep.

Halfway through the night, the King had a dream, in that dream he had a large family as a King and then passed away. He is then born in the house of sewer-cleaners (referred to as Chandals) who are of low social standing. He gets married and has children, but here too he dies and then he wakes up from the dream. He is shocked and thinks *"What happened in the dream? Will this truly happen when I die? Oh, deeds of mine (Karma) will you take me to such a lowly existence? Why have I sinned so much! Now, Guru Jee you will tell me what this all means."* Scratching his head confused, he then falls asleep again.

The King went hunting with his entourage the next day. Guru Sahib accompanied him. Even though the King was jovial and enjoying the sport of the hunt, his mind kept going back to the terrifying nightmare that he had, had. He thought dreams are just that, just dreams. But his mind still kept thinking of the dream. The King travelled out far during the hunt and went after a deer – he lost everyone else in his pursuit of the deer. He grew tired and now sat down under a tree to rest.

Near this tree was the house of some Chandals. A ten year old boy started to stare at the King, he ran away to his mother and said, *"Father, is sitting under that tree, he is still alive and wearing expensive clothes."* The boy's mother came and shouted at the King, *"Let's go home. How have you become wealthy?"* (referring to his expensive clothing).

The King was perplexed as this was the same family he had seen in the dream. Soon, the whole family gathered and all of them were saying, *"Come home."* The King refused to go and tried to scare them, but they were not listening. He was confused as he knew the family from his dream, he could not fathom how the people in the dream could exist in reality and are standing in front of him.

Guru Jee arrived along with their Sikhs and the whole entourage from the hunting expedition. The Chandals also recognised Guru Jee and begged, *"Oh Guru Jee, please help us, our whole family is suffering in poverty, while he is having the time of his life"* (being wealthy, referring to the King, who they were convinced was their family member). Guru Jee asked, *"Where did you bury your beloved (deceased)."* The family replied, *"We buried him four days ago."* Guru Jee said, *"Let's go and dig up the grave. If your beloved is still buried, then this King is at no fault other than that he looks like your relative who deceased."* Everyone agreed with this and made their way to the grave, the family's relative was still present in the grave. The relatives asked for forgiveness and left to

God is realised by the True Guru's Grace

go back to their village. The King and Guru Jee returned too. The next day the King came to Guru Jee when they were sitting peacefully. The King asked Guru Jee, *"True King, what was my dream? How did the dream manifest into reality? How did the conflict of the dream and reality (the dead person looking exactly like the King) also get resolved?"*

Guru Jee replied, *"King! This was all in answer to your question, from a few days back. Your karma (destiny of deeds committed) was such that you were born in the house of Chandals. For your previous actions you were to undergo this life of a Chandal, that life has now been abolished by it occurring in a dream for you. You saw this in reality too and that grief has been abolished. So you still underwent the destiny written. But what you were to undergo in a lifetime has been undergone whilst sleeping/dreaming for a few minutes and whilst awake yesterday. It has thus been undergone. God's sanctuary is such that it has the power to do such things. Karma starts with your birth, they also have an end. All things that have a beginning, have an end too. Only God has no start and no end. You believe in Karma to be eternal, this is incorrect. Karma begun with the birth of the living being and so forth, people carried on creating karma. But, these karma will also end as they are not permanent but temporary. By obeying God's command(s) your karma gets abolished. You come to the world through God's command. Now, by obeying these commands, enshrining the truth and righteousness into your life, these karma can get expelled. The fragrance of God's power will wash away your sinful actions, it will permeate your life, when you obey God.* Sri Guru Nanak Dev Jee says,

The One Name is my lamp; I have put the oil of suffering into it. It's flame has dried up this oil, and I have escaped my meeting with the Messenger of Death. ||1|| O people, do not make fun of me. Thousands of wooden logs, piled up together, need only a tiny flame to burn. (Ang, 358)

The power of God and meditation upon Naam can and does transform our lives.

9. Harmander Sahib & Amritsar Sarovar Seva

The construction of Harmander Sahib was now fully underway and many Sikhs came to participate in its construction. Many stories about their Seva and the inspirational nature of their relationships with Guru Jee have been narrated by Bhai Vir Singh in his book 'Jeevan Parsang Sri Guru Arjan Dev Jee' – from where a lot of this information in these preliminary chapters has been translated from. To keep the book short – I have not translated many of these historical incidents – so those that can read Punjabi are urged to also read that book in full.

Many historical signs of this Seva (devotional voluntary service) of construction are still present today. As earlier mentioned the 'Ber Baba Buddha Jee' the tree under which Baba Jee sat and supervised the construction can be seen on the right hand corner of the Sarovar after entering the complex from the main clock tower entrance. Near the entrance to the walkway to Harmander Sahib (the path to it) on the right hand side is the 'Lachi Ber' where there now is Sri Guru Granth Sahib Jee in a room – it was at this spot that Sri Guru Arjan Dev Jee supervised the construction. Guru Jee would also come and sit and watch the construction from where now stands 'Thara Sahib'. This is the platform on the left hand side of the 'Dukh Bhanjnee Ber' (tree that eradicates disease). A Gurdwara used to stand at this spot to mark Guru Jee sitting here but it was demolished by the Akalis (administration of the Shiromani Gurdwara Parbhandak Committee) the platform was then reinstated when Sant Lakhbir Singh of Bakapur protested at the destruction of this historical site as did the Sikh masses. Then the current structure was constructed and the marble Palki

God is realised by the True Guru's Grace

Sahib (palanquin) now signifies the point of where Guru Jee would sit.

Further on, is what is now called 'Manji Sahib' this is on the left towards the exit (near the Langar Hall) – it is a large hall now and is where daily Hukamnama katha (discourse of the daily command of the Guru) takes place. It was here that Maharaj used to take rest under some trees.

To teach us that God is present everywhere – Harmander Sahib was built with four doorways (showing God's presence in all directions). Also the four doorways were all built in the middle of a compass direction, so the doorways are at north-east, north-west, south-east and south-west. This signified God's pervasive nature in all directions and a non-rigid nature.

The steps and walls of the Sarovar were all made permanent, thus they were firmed up and reinforced in the construction. Harmander Sahib was purposely kept at a lower level than the outside streets levels of Ramdaspur. This was done to show you have to be humble to realise God. Harmander Sahib was constructed in the centre with no ceiling for the first floor (with a balcony above) but at the rear, a ceiling was constructed over the 'Har Kee Pauri' (the spot were God did Seva – baskets were seen floating by themselves with debris during the construction). In this way Harmander Sahib was constructed and alongside this, the city of Ramdaspur kept on developing too.

Visiting Sikhs would say 'Great is Sri Guru Arjan Dev Jee who constructed such a splendid Harmander Sahib.' Guru Jee would humbly respond by saying this it is down to the grace and work of God to construct and establish such a place where God does reside in full spiritual splendour.

Guru Jee described the construction with the following Shabad,

God has stood up to resolve the affairs of Saints; coming in person to complete their tasks. The land is beautiful (of Ramdaspur), and the pool is beautiful (the Sarovar); within it is contained the Ambrosial Water (Immortal nectar). The Ambrosial Water is filling it, God has helped me complete the task at hand (building Harmander Sahib and the Sarovar); all my desires are fulfilled. Congratulations are pouring in from all over the world; all my sorrows are eliminated. The Vedas and the Puraanas sing the Praises of the Perfect, Unchanging, Imperishable Primal Lord. The exalted creator - God has kept to His innate nature; Nanak thus meditates on His name (in gratitude). ||1|| The Creator has given me the nine treasures, wealth and spiritual powers, and I do not lack anything. Eating, spending and enjoying, I have found peace; the gifts of the Creator Lord continually increase. His gifts increase and shall never be exhausted; I have found the Inner-knower of hearts. Millions of obstacles have all been removed, and grief does not come near me. Tranquillity, peace, poise and bliss prevail in abundance, and all my desires are abolished. Nanak sings the Glorious Praises of his Lord and Master, whose Glorious Greatness is wonderful and amazing. ||2|| It was God's job, and God has done it; what can the mere mortal do? The devotees are adorned, singing the Glorious Praises of the Lord; they proclaim God's eternal victory. Singing the Glorious Praises of the Lord of the Universe, bliss wells up, and we are friends with the Saadh Sangat, the

Company of the Holy. He who made the effort to construct this sacred pool (Amritsar) - how can his praises be recounted? The merits of the sixty-eight sacred shrines of pilgrimage, charity, good deeds and immaculate lifestyle, are found in this sacred pool. It is the natural way of the Lord and Master to purify sinners; Nanak takes the Support of the Word of the Shabad. ||3|| The treasure of virtue is my God, the Creator Lord; what Praises of Yours should I sing, O Lord? The prayer of the Saints is, "O Lord and Master, please bless us with the supreme, sublime essence of Your Name." Please, grant us Your Name, grant us this blessing, and do not forget us, even for an instant. Chant the Glorious Praises of the World-Lord, O my tongue; sing them forever, night and day. One who enshrines love for the Naam, the Name of the Lord, his mind and body are drenched with Ambrosial Nectar. Prays Nanak, my desires have been fulfilled; gazing upon the Blessed Vision of the Lord, I live. ||4||7||10|| (Sohee, 783)

This Shabad was also the first Hukamnama (order taken for guidance) received from Sri Aadh Granth too (to be described in the preceding chapters).

Guru Jee made this 'Harmander', which translates to 'Temple of God,' where only God is meditated upon for every second of the day. It is also a centre of God consciousness in which one's ego is left at the door. One has to walk down the steps to get to this temple of God. In God consciousness we have no ego and realise God is the doer and power behind everything.

This is the only Gurdwara where the word 'temple' is used as an accurate translation, usually temples refer to places where praying to angels/deities takes place – a practice the Guru's were against but they made this the 'Temple of God' where only God is meditated upon.

So now, the Harmander Sahib and Sarovar had been constructed along with the walkway to Harmander Sahib – this had all been achieved with the grace of God. The township of Ramdaspur had also expanded in commerce and a city was now growing continually. The scene was described in Gurbani by Sri Guru Arjan Dev Jee:

I have seen all places, but none compare to you (Harmander Sahib). The Primal Lord, the Architect of Destiny, has established You; thus You are adorned and embellished. Ramdaspur is prosperous and thickly populated, and incomparably beautiful. O Lord! Bathing in the Sacred Pool of Raam Dass, sins are washed away, O Nanak. ||10|| (1361)

Now, services for the congregation began at Harmander Sahib with Asa Dee Var Kirtan starting before 3am and the place to hit the gong (Ghareeaal) had been made permanent outside the doors of the Darshani Deori (entrance to walkway to Harmander Sahib). The playing of the gong alerted the local residents of the time of day. This has now been lost to history, it used to be played near where the two Nishaan Sahibs (Sikh flags) are now. There used to be a room there (near the Nishan Sahibs) from where the gong would be played near what is now the exit or stairs (where now stands the June 1984 Shaheed Ganj Gurdwara). During the Asa Dee Vaar, Guru Jee would arrive and be seated in Harmander Sahib. Nowadays, Sri Guru Granth Sahib Jee arrives at the same time.

When the whole of the construction was complete, a thanks giving service was held in which God was thanked for blessing humanity with such a temple of God. At this time Guru Jee also showered blessings upon all the Sikhs who had participated in the Seva. The main responsibilities of the construction project had been carried out by Baba Buddha Jee, Bhai Bhagta Jee and Bhai Behlo Jee.

Baba Buddha Jee was already very respected from the times of Sri Guru Nanak Dev Jee – he was given boons of being liberated and to be forever devout and one who will always be of assistance to the congregation. Bhai Bhagta Jee was also given liberation immediately – so he was fully God conscious and made the leader of the Baraars (Sikhs from a certain area). Bhai Bhagta was given divine wisdom and given secret powers. Other Sikhs who were blessed by Maharaj for conducting the Seva were Bhai Ugru Jee, Bhai Kalyana Jee, Bhai Ajab Jee, Bhai Ajaib Jee, Bhai Umarshah Jee, Bhai Sangha Jee, Bhai Paira Jee, Bhai Langaha Jee and Bhai Salo Jee. Bhai Salo Jee was made the head of the township of Ramdaspur and in charge of the administration. In this way the thanksgiving program concluded.

Laying the foundation stone of Harmander Sahib

When Sri Guru Arjan Dev Jee had placed the first brick down to lay the foundation for Harmander Sahib the chief bricklayer lifted it and placed it back down, in line with his preference. Guru Jee smiled at this and said, *"The foundation stone for the eternal temple should have also remained unmoveable but it has now moved. We will see the effect of this in the future."* These words became true when Ahmed Shah Abdali demolished Harmander

Sahib by using explosives in 1762 CE, 2 years later in 1764 rebuilt Harmander Sahib from the original bricks (that could be recovered). Today's Golden version of Harmander Sahib with marble works was constructed by Maharaja Ranjit Singh in 1802 CE. During the Misl period and that of Maharaja Ranjit Singh, Sikh Leaders (Sardars) gave expensive gifts encrusted with jewels which are still in the toshkhana (stores of Harmander Sahibs most expensive items) and are displayed on auspicious occasions, this display is called 'Jalao.'

The centre of Sikhi

Harmander Sahib became the centre of Sikh affairs – it became the heartbeat of Sikhs – the most sacred Gurdwara. Generations upon generations of Sikhs have all attempted to make Haramder Sahib more extravagant – the love of Sikhs, honour and respect is all centred in Harmander Sahib. This will always remain the supreme temple of God. The preaching of Sikhi is central to the fame, glory and sacredness of Harmander Sahib.

In this temple only God can be mediated upon and nothing else. Rejuvenating and non-stop recitals take place. The singing of Gurbani emanates from Harmander Sahib, under the canopy of Sri Guru Granth Sahib Jee's magical aura. Even when Sri Guru Granth Sahib Jee is not present on the ground floor, and cleaning takes place – recitals of Gurbani continue on the first and second floors where Akhand Paaths (recitals of Sri Guru Granth Sahib Jee) continue and the sevadaars also continuously meditate whilst doing Seva in Harmander Sahib. Externally on the edge of the Sarovar or in its surrounds, you can always find people meditating or doing recitals of Gurbani, at all times of the day and night. These rays of

God is realised by the True Guru's Grace

God's name keep the Harmander Sahib booming with spiritual energy at all times.

Harmander Sahib is like a lotus in the Sarovar of Amritsar. By coming to this lotus one is lifted from the worldly worries they are in and realise the spirit within. Many people from the globe over come to seek spiritual rejuvenation. People from all walks of life, of all faiths, attain peace upon visiting, their wishes are fulfilled, their ailments are cured, by sitting here and bathing in Amritsar. Many cases of people being cured here can be found by simple internet searches – many leave cured and only a few share their stories. The work of God continues in silence, mostly, whilst people's prayers and wishes are fulfilled even with one visit.

finding our way back home, to the Palace of love ♥

10. Bhai Hema

Guru Sahib went to do parchar in many villages near Amritsar and after being at the village Khapur they arrived at what now is 'Tarn Taran.' There were only five Sikhs with Guru Jee, outside the village Maharaj sat under a tree and became absorbed in meditation. In the evening it started raining and no one came from the village to offer Maharaj shelter/accommodation. It seems like all the villagers were followers of the Muslim Pir (Saint) Sakhi Sarvar. Bhai Biddhi Chand asked Guru Jee, *"Grant me permission to enter the village and find us somewhere to stay (in shelter)."* Guru Jee replied, *"No remain seated here, rely on the will of God, it will be of benefit to us"*. But, Bhai Biddhi Chand repeatedly asked for permission to enter the village and Guru Jee agreed in the end. When he entered the village no-one spoke to Bhai Biddhi Chand and if they did, they teased him rather than offer support to be accommodated. He returned and Guru Jee said, *"Stay here seated, God is the one who provides, God will send someone."*

Now, a Sikh approached them, he was called Hema. He lived outside the village, he supplicated to Guru Jee, *"Oh True Guru, this slave of yours has a very humble home which is tatty and in need of repairs – it is not suitable for you. But if you could go there, take rest – this will give me much joy, as my Master then would be sitting in shelter, otherwise the situation is not good, that I remain seated under shelter and you and my brothers remain here exposed in the rain."* Seeing his devotion Maharaj got up and left to go to his humble abode and rested there. Bhai Hema cooked whatever food he could muster and offered it to Maharaj and the Sikhs to eat. Guru Jee wrote the following shabad describing this Sikhs devotion to God even though he lived in poverty:

He dwells in a broken-down shack, in tattered clothes, with no social status, no honor and no respect; he wanders in the wilderness, with no friend or lover, without wealth, beauty, relatives or relations. Even so, he is the king of the whole world, if his mind is imbued with the Lord's Name. With the dust of his feet, men are redeemed, because God is very pleased with him. (707)

Guru Jee stayed here in Bhai Hema's humble abode for a few days and fulfilled Bhai Hema's desire to serve Guru Jee. His wish was that he passed away in the feet of the Guru. He was a perfected spiritualist and knew he was to pass away soon and his final wish was to now pass, whilst at the feet of the Guru. One day he bowed at Guru Jee's feet and said, *"Now make us one."* In this way, Bhai Hema passed away in the feet of the Guru. Guru Jee did his funeral and went on to the village Khaara.

11. Khaara & Tarn Taran

The village Khaara was in beautiful scenic surrounds, surrounded by trees, fruit trees of Mangoes, Ber (Punjabi Jujube), Jamanu (Punjabi blackberry), peaches and beetroot were present. The villagers went to much effort to accommodate Guru Jee in the most respectful manner.

A Gurdwara now marks this visit of Guru Jee at village Khaara. A well is present as well as a pool of water which was purified by Guru Jee washing their feet in it. This is called 'Dukh Nivaran' which translates to the place that dispels grief/disease.

Guru Jee was already aware, but now also saw how people in this vicinity were converting to Islam under the influence of the rulers. In these villages around Khaara, Sikhi (the Sikh faith) was also flourishing but Guru Jee felt a central place of worship needed to be constructed to bring all these villagers together in worship. For this reason, Guru Jee was looking for a suitable site for this to occur. A plot of land was thus purchased which now houses Darbar Sahib Gurdwara of Tarn Taran.

Guru Sahib started the construction work for the Sarovar at Tarn Taran, labourers were employed. Sikhs came from neighbouring villages and far off to do Seva and the Sarovar excavations were conducted. The land was purchased and excavated for the Sarovar in the years 1590 – 1591 CE. In 1596 CE the bricks were to be laid for the construction and a government official called Noor Deen stole all the bricks (some sources say it was his son

Amir Deen who did this). He was building his government rest house nearby and used the bricks to build it.

The Sikhs said a complaint to the Emperor should be made but Guru Jee refused their appeal and said, *"What God has willed is correct, what happened is in God's will, it will be for our benefit."* It is also stated by historians that Guru Jee had said *"These same bricks will one day be used to reinforce the Sarovar."* This became true in 1766 CE when Jassa Singh Ramgharia demolished Noor Deen's rest house and used the bricks in reclamation works of the Sarovar. Others who also did Seva of Tarn Taran Darbar Sahib include Maharaja Ranjit Singh, Prince Naunihal Singh, Bhai Hakam Singh and many others Sikhs from the Sikh nation. Sant Sham Singh of Amritsar got the gold leaf added.

Even though Noor Deen had stolen the bricks – the construction continued and the Sarovar remained an earthen structure and the water of the Sarovar kept a milky complexion (due to clay in the earth). Where there is now a marble and gold encrusted Gurdwara of Darbar Sahib at Tarn Taran, initially a small Gurdwara was built and a monthly congregation was held on Masiya (day of no-moon). In the area of Majha this became the centre of Sikhs and people who had developed desires of renouncing worldly attachment started to reside on the outskirts of the Sarovar.

At some distance from here a home for lepers was established. This home grew over time. During the Sikh Raj of Maharaja Ranjit Singh and the 'Misls' (Sikh confederate rule) a government grant was given and during the times of the colonial rule of the British the homes administration was taken over by Christians.

12. The congregation of Agra

A congregation had come from Agra to have the blessed company of Sri Guru Arjan Dev Jee. They asked a question about being householders and how they could become liberated, as people from traditions of renouncing the world, had told them salvation was not possible as a householder (married with children and so on). Guru Jee laughed at their question and replied, *"You are married and are only a husband and wife, get married to another three or four women and your salvation will be assured."* Everyone was shocked with his reply and said, *"Maharaj, being married to one wife is a struggle – how can we marry another three or four?"* Guru Jee smiled and said, *"The four wives you have mentioned, you are to marry them with your mind, not physically, listen carefully and understand what is meant by this:*

1. Make **mercy** an internal characteristic of your mind - a 'wife' who is always there for you. So, when you see someone in poverty, in grief, with less virtue than yourself, in need, someone less powerful; do not feel sorrow for them, do not discriminate against them, or treat them badly. Be merciful and help that person.

2. Create an outlook of **friendliness** to all – this is the second wife to marry to your mind. If you see somebody with more wealth, education, virtues, happiness, respect than you; love that person, see him/her as a second self. Do not be jealous of that person.

3. Be happy, take on a **positive outlook** at all times. Make this a constant virtue. So, if you see someone

more powerful than you, with more virtues, more education, happier, wealthier, more devout, more charitable; be happy upon their sight; be grateful you have met someone better than yourself. If you get time, benefit from their company.

4. Take an outlook of seeing someone as a **'stranger.'** Give that outlook a place in your mind as a wife. So if you meet somebody, upon whom none of the three above mentioned traits have effect on and if the person still takes on the wrong path, even after good advice – do not have enmity or animosity with them. Rather, treat them like somebody you do not know, like a stranger, leave them be. For example, in a shopping centre we walk past many strangers, we are neither their friends nor enemies. In the same way you can treat this person like a stranger.

When you take on these virtues, then your meditation and bliss of it, will no longer be effected with your worldly interactions. All your meditations will bear eternal fruit (they will no longer be expunged by sinful acts) and you will experience nirvana whilst being householders.

When we live householder's lives and also try to be spiritual, we sometimes develop bad traits which are obstacles to our spiritual progression they are:

- Discrimination – against those less spiritually progressed;

- Jealousy against those who are content and happy;

- Burning ego – when we see others progressing more than us;

- Enmity – sometimes those we help, develop enmity against us, or we just develop enmity against someone else."

The solutions for these four problems have already been given in the aforementioned virtues.

***

13. Kartarpur of Doaba

In 1593 CE to decrease the animosity with Prithi Chand, Sri Guru Arjan Dev Jee left Ramdaspur and went to Tarn Taran. Tarn Taran developed into a township and people started to reside there. As it was a central location, the surrounding villagers now found a place to get their commodities, as traders set up there. Maharaj stayed here for a while and then toured other villages and arrived at village Dalla, where many devout Sikhs lived. Whilst staying here the lead government official of Jalandhar came to have a sight of Guru Jee, as he had heard their praises, his name was Azeem Khan. After seeing Guru Sahib he was rapt with peace. In the Langar, he saw that people of all castes, religions and wealth, were treated equally; fed in the same manner without any discrimination. He also listened to the teachings of Guru Jee. His heart was racing with joy with what he saw.

One day Azeem Khan asked Guru Jee, *"Is there a difference in Muslims and Hindus? Their forms of worship are different. Who do you worship? What differences do you see between them?"* Guru Jee answered with the following Shabad (some of the meanings of the following Shabad will be lost in translation, as the words used in the original Gurmukhi, give a different connotation of the

God is realised by the True Guru's Grace

words used by Hindus and Muslims in their scriptures and practices as opposed to the English translations);

"God is the doer; the cause of causes; the bountiful Lord. The merciful Lord sustains all. The Lord is unseen, indescribable and infinite (words used by Hindus to describe God). God is great and endless (words used by Muslims to describe God). I humbly pray to invoke the universal Lord God, the Lord of the world (Hindus describe God like this). The creator Lord is all-pervading, everywhere. (Muslims describe God like this). 1. Pause and contemplate (these meanings). He is the Lord of the universe, the life of the world, the husband Lord of 'Maya,' illusion (as described by Hindus). Within your heart, worship and adore the destroyer of fear. God is the Master of the senses; Lord and cherisher of the World. He is perfect, ever-present everywhere, the Liberator. ||2||God you are the one and only merciful master; spiritual teacher; prophet; religious teacher. God is the master of hearts; dispenser of justice; more sacred than the Quran and other Semitic scriptures. ||3|| The Lord is described by Hindus as the powerful 'NarSingh' (half lion, half man) and merciful. The all-pervading Lord is the support of each and every heart. The luminous Lord dwells everywhere. God's play cannot be known. ||4|| Be kind and compassionate to me, O Creator Lord. Bless me with devotion and meditation, O Lord Creator. Says Nanak, the Guru has rid me of doubt. The Muslim God 'Allah' and the Hindu God 'Paarbrahm' are one and the same. (896)

After hearing this Shabad he was satisfied and understood what Guru Jee taught.

After congregating with Maharaj for a few days, his faith increased and he became a follower of Guru Jee. He then asked Maharaj to come and live somewhere near Jalandhar, as coming to Dalla was far for him to travel.

Guru Jee agreed to do this. So on the 21st of Maghar (Bikrami Calendar month) 1594 CE he acquired a place for Maharaj to reside at. Some historical accounts argue that Guru Jee brought the land outright to establish Kartarpur. Maybe Azeem Khan assisted in purchasing the land, in that way – both versions can be correct. In a few days a township started to spring up and Guru Jee named it 'Kartarpur' – 'the place of the creator God.' Guru Jee returned to Amritsar after some months here.

***

14. Birth of Sri Guru Hargobind Sahib Jee

Even though Sri Guru Arjan Dev Jee made many efforts to keep on good terms with his elder brother Prithi Chand, they had no effect he carried on with his animosity. He celebrated the upcoming arrival of his friend Sulhi Khan to Ramdaspur, with much pomp and fanfare.

Guru Jee was already in discussions with leading Sikhs, as to what should be done next, to avoid conflict. It was collectively decided in 1594 CE that Guru Jee and all the leading Sikhs, would now go and reside 4km away from Harmander Sahib at Vadali (which is now called Sultanwind): where the villagers were devout Sikhs. Guru Jee was housed in a beautiful Haveli (country-house). Many came and lived here and Sikh congregations started to come directly here and daily services began to be held.

Many left Ramdaspur and went to Vadali. Some of the remaining Sikhs heard that Sulhi Khan would loot and steal their belongings – so they too went and moved out to far away places.

Sulhi Khan arrived but he could not loot or plunder the people. He asked Prithi Chand what had gone wrong and Prithi Chand said, *"Upon hearing of your arrival he ran away (referring to Guru Jee) and so did most of the local residents."* Prithi Chand said he will get the town populated again and doesn't think Guru Jee will return but if he does he will ask Sulhi Khan for assistance. Sulhi Khan left and attended to the governments tasks he had came for and went back to Delhi.

Now, Prithi Chand had complete control of Ramdaspur and he would burn day and night as very little donations were made, so income was sparse. He wanted more wealth and praise in the world. Upon learning that Sikhs were still flocking to his younger brother Guru Jee, Prithi Chand would burn with envy and rage. He wanted to become the light of the world, like the sun but was only a dim lamp.

In contrast, Guru Jee at Vadali was acting in the spirit of Sri Guru Nanak – helping all who visited. He dispelled people's doubts and their wishes were fulfilled. All visitors would leave Vadali care-free. Guru Jee set up a well at Chheharta Sahib which is about 1 Km from Vadali and gave boons for bathing with its waters, saying all sins could get erased and those wishing for offspring should bathe here monthly to fulfil their desire.

In 1595 here at Vadali, Mata Ganga Jee gave birth to Sri Hargobind Sahib Jee the only son of Sri Guru Arjan Dev Jee and on the auspicious occasion of this birth, Guru Jee uttered the following Shabads,

"The True Guru has sent a child. The long-lived one has been born into this destiny with the boon of Baba Buddha

God is realised by the True Guru's Grace

Jee. He came to acquire a home in the womb, and his mother's heart was ecstatic. ||1|| A son is born - a devotee of the cherisher of the Universe (God). This pre-ordained destiny has been revealed to all. Pause and contemplate (upon this). In the tenth month (after completion of nine months), by the Lord's Order, the baby has been born. Sorrow is dispelled, and great joy has ensued. The companions blissfully sing the songs of the Guru's Bani to celebrate. This is pleasing to the Lord Master. ||2|| The vine has grown, and shall last for many generations. The power of Dharma (righteousness) has been firmly established by the Lord. That which my mind wishes for, the True Guru has granted. I have become carefree, and I fix my attention on the One Lord. ||3|| As the child places so much faith in his father, I speak as it pleases the Guru to have me speak. This is not a hidden secret; Guru Nanak, greatly pleased, has bestowed this gift. (396)

The transcendent Lord has brought bliss to all; confirming His innate nature. God has become Merciful to the humble, holy Saints, and all my relatives blossom forth in joy. ||1|| The True Guru Himself has resolved my affairs. He has blessed Hargobind with long life, and taken care of my comfort, happiness and well-being. ||1||Pause and contemplate (upon this). The forests, meadows and the three worlds have blossomed forth in greenery; God gives support to all beings. Nanak has obtained the fruits of his mind's desires; his desires are totally fulfilled." (806)

Celebrations took place at Vadali upon the birth of this divine baby. Many Sikhs travelled in, to join the festivities and forty days passed like this.

Whilst in the house of Prithi Chand, an atmosphere of sadness prevailed. Prithi Chand paid a midwife to add poison to her teats and go to Vadali and try poisoning the newborn baby, in order to murder him. He paid her 100 rupees. She arrived on the fortieth day after the birth, when festivities were taking place. She wore expensive clothes and came dressed as a wealthy person and took the baby into her arms. She tried breastfeeding the baby, but the baby squeezed the breast with one hand and pulled at her plait with the other hand. She screamed in agony and begged for forgiveness. Whilst lying down, dying there, she told everyone what had happened – the poison had entered her body by the squeezing of the baby and she died there in agony.

All the Sikhs at Vadali were astounded at this evil attempt of assassination. People were cursing Prithi Chand; his wife Karmo; and the midwife. Others were praising Sri Guru Arjan Dev Jee's power – which had ensured the baby was safe. The baby was also a great spiritualist, born with all powers of divinity who had defended himself, even if he was just days old.

Sri Arjan Dev Jee arrived at the scene and witnessed the midwife dead and the atmosphere of shock in the household. He saw a worried Mata Ganga Jee and said, *"Do not be worried. This is all the grace of the perfect Sri Guru Nanak Dev Jee that we have been saved of any mishap, concentrate upon Him. Why do we worry of the future, if He protected us now, He will protect is in the future too."* Guru Jee ordered the making of Karah Parshad (out of gratitude) and got ink and a pen and wrote the following Shabad.

Giving His Hand, the Perfect Guru has protected the child. The glory of His servant (Hargobind the baby) has become manifest. ||1|| I contemplate the Guru, the enlightener; I meditate on the Guru, the enlightener. I offer my heart-felt prayer to the Guru, and it is answered. Pause and contemplate (upon this). I have taken to the Sanctuary of the True Divine Guru. The service of His servant has been fulfilled. ||2|| He has preserved my soul, body, youth and life breath (praan). Says Nanak, I am a sacrifice to the Guru. (396)

***

Historical accounts say that Sri Guru Arjan Dev Jee left Vadali in 1597 CE. It is not clear what happens in the 7 years between 1597-1604 CE, we know Sri Aadh Granth gets compiled by 1604 CE. But other than that I have not found much other information for this time period and it is not clear of what the relationship with Prithi Chand was like and how after leaving Ramdaspur Guru Jee regained the administration of Harmander Sahib from Prithi Chand. If further information of this seven year period is learnt of I will add it to future editions of this book.

The following chapter will be about the compilation of Sri Aadh Granth, the time period taken to compile the Granth is not mentioned historically but one would assume at least about 1 year to complete the project.

God is realised by the True Guru's Grace

15. Baba Mohan Jee & Gurbani

Sri Guru Nanak Dev Jee when anointing Sri Guru Angad Dev Jee as the second Guru had said, "Create a nation." This meant building upon the foundations of nation-building that Sri Guru Nanak Dev Jee had started for Sikhs. These foundations were of truth, Naam (scripture), altruism and defeating one's ego to become enlightened. The aim was to realise the pervasiveness of God and then work for the betterment of all. In this manner each Guru instructed the next Guru to build upon the development of the Sikh nation.

As part of this nation building Sri Guru Arjan Dev Jee had built Harmander Sahib which is the most sacred Gurdwara for Sikhs. Now, Guru Sahib wanted to collate all the hymns authored by the previous Guru's and compile a Granth (anthology). Sri Guru Angad Dev Jee had collated all the writings of Sri Guru Nanak Dev Jee and during the times of Sri Guru Amar Das Jee all the writings of the Guru's were collated into two Pothia (anthologies). These pothia were in the possession of Baba Mohan Jee the eldest son of Sri Guru Amar Das Jee (the third Guru). Now, Sri Guru Arjan Dev Jee wanted to collate these two pothia with the works of Sri Guru Ram Dass Jee, their own writings and the writings of other enlightened souls (Sikhs and non-Sikhs) to make a new singular Granth.

To commence the compilation of the new Granth – the pothia held at Goindval with Baba Mohan Jee had to be acquired. Bhai Gurdas Jee volunteered to go to Goindval to obtain the Pothia. He arrived one day at about midday at Goindval with this task in mind. He first did an ishnaan (bathed) in the Baoli Sahib (blessed well with 84

God is realised by the True Guru's Grace

steps leading to it) and then proceeded to the home of Baba Mohan Jee.

When Bhai Gurdas Jee arrived at the home of Baba Mohan Jee the front door to the house was locked from inside, thus somebody was home. Bhai Gurdas Jee knocked the door but nobody answered, thus he sat outside the door and started to supplicate to Baba Mohan Jee to come out and open the door, calling him out. Inside the house Baba Mohan Jee was in a meditative trance, imbued in meditation and completely unaware of Bhai Gurdas Jee outside.

Bhai Gurdas Jee sat outside the door to Baba Mohan Jee's house and made pleas for the Pothia all night long, but the doors to the house never opened. Eventually, Bhai Gurdas Jee became disheartened and left. Upon his return to Ramdaspur, Bhai Gurdas Jee narrated what had happened.

Now, Baba Buddha Jee sought permission to go to Goindval and obtain the Pothia. Guru Sahib gave him permission and he left for Goindval. Upon arrival he too did ishnaan first at Baoli Sahib and then proceeded to the home of Baba Mohan Jee. The door was locked from inside and Baba Buddha Jee shouted for Baba Mohan Jee to open the door, he made continuous supplications for a while but to no avail, there were no signs of the door opening. Baba Buddha Jee then started to shake the front doors forcefully and this led to movement in the frame of the doors, Baba Jee then removed some bricks around the door frame and unlatched the doors and entered the house.

Upon entering the home of Baba Mohan Jee, Baba Buddha Jee saw that Baba Mohan Jee was in a meditative trance with no consciousness of his physical body. His body was not moving; it was completely still and transfixed in meditation.

Baba Mohri Jee, Baba Mohan Jee's younger brother had heard the noise from the doors being forced open and he arrived at the scene. He ordered Baba Buddha Jee to not stir Baba Mohan Jee and not break his meditation; he warned he would curse him if he did touch him. He said it was wrong of Baba Buddha Jee to also force entry into the house. Baba Buddha Jee left after hearing this and seeing Baba Mohan Jee in his meditative trance. Upon his return he narrated what had happened.

Now, Guru Jee themselves left for Goindval. Upon arrival they too bathed at Baoli Sahib, sat down and started to meditate, they became imbued in their meditation. Sri Guru Amar Das Jee appeared (gave darshan) and gave words of advice to Sri Guru Arjan Dev Jee whilst they meditated saying, *"You will get the Pothia but will have to listen to harsh words, do not react to them, tolerate them."* After getting this advice Sri Guru Arjan Dev Jee made his way to Baba Mohan Jee's home.

Sri Guru Arjan Dev Jee had a mandolin (instrument like a guitar) in their hand, they walked barefooted (showing humility) and went and sat outside Baba Mohan Jee's house. Guru Jee didn't allow the Sikhs to put a spread out for them to sit on and they sat on the dusty floor as it was. They then started playing the mandolin and sang this Shabad in a melodic voice,

"O Mohan, your room is so lofty (his room was on the highest floor of the house called a 'Chubara'), and your house is unsurpassed. O Mohan, your doors to your home are beautiful. They are the worship-houses of the Saints. In

these incomparable worship-houses, the singing of Kirtan occurs at all times; praising God. This is where the Saints and the Holy gather together there they meditate on you-God. Be kind and compassionate, O merciful Lord; be merciful to the meek. Prays Nanak, I thirst for the blessed vision of Your Darshan (sight of God and Baba Mohan in this instance); receiving Your Darshan, I am totally at peace." (248)

Baba Mohan Jee's meditative state had not been moved in the two previous attempts, but today the sound of melodic Gurbani sung by Guru Jee broke his meditation. Baba Mohan Jee opened a window and looked out into the alley and saw it was Guru Jee singing, he spoke harsh words when he saw Guru Jee. The melodic Gurbani being sung continued nonetheless and now Guru Jee sang the following lines,

"O Mohan, your speech is incomparable; wondrous are your ways. O Mohan, you believe in the One God. Everything else is dust to you. You adore the One Lord, the unknowable Lord and master; whose power gives support to all. Through the Guru's word, you have captured the heart of the primal being, the Lord of the world. You yourself move, and you yourself stand still; you yourself support the whole creation. Prays Nanak, please preserve my honor; all your servants seek the protection of your sanctuary." (248)

Hearing this Baba Mohan Jee became benevolent and melted after hearing his own praise, in response to the harsh words he had spoken. He recognised the wisdom of Guru Jee and regretted speaking harshly and thought he should now serve Guru Jee with devotion. He realised how peaceful Guru Jee was, even whilst he insulted them. Realising how perfect Guru Jee was Baba Mohan Jee now wanted to give them the Pothia, in line with the wishes of his father (Sri Guru Amar Das Jee) as Sri Guru Arjan Dev Jee was their successor. Baba Mohan Jee came out of his house and praised Guru Jee. In response Sri Guru Arjan Dev Jee sung the following Shabad,

"O Mohan, the congregation of the holy, meditates on you; they meditate on the blessed vision of you. Mohan, the messenger of death does not even approach those who meditate on you (God), at the last moment. The messenger of death cannot touch those who meditate on you (God) single-mindedly. Those who worship and adore you (God) in thought, word and deed, obtain all fruits and rewards. Those who are stupid and filthy with urine they become all-knowing upon gaining your blessed vision (sight of God - darshan). Says Nanak, your kingdom is eternal, O perfect primal Lord God." (248)

Guru Jee had his eyes closed and was imbued in singing God's praises (the above Shabads relates to both a situational context of being at the door of Baba Mohan Jee but also relates to God, one of the words used to describe God in Gurbani is 'Mohan' too, which means fascinating). Baba Mohan Jee saw the love of God that Guru Jee had and recognised Guru Jee as an enlightened being who is one with God. Baba Mohan Jee presented the Pothia and bowed at the feet of Guru Jee. Seeing this the fountain of humility Sri Guru Arjan Dev Jee said, *"You are an elder of mine, you are my Mama (maternal uncle), Sri Guru Amar Das Jee was your father, please do not bow to me."*

Baba Mohan Jee said, *"You are the son of my sister and I should touch your feet as I have sinned, please forgive me."* Guru Jee forgave him and blessed him with boons that he should be freed of all grief in human life and thereafter.

Guru Jee arose to leave with the Pothia but now Baba Mohri Jee stopped them from leaving, lovingly taking Guru Jee to meet the rest of the relatives at Goindval. Everyone was ecstatic at meeting Guru Jee and they stayed on for another night here.

Baba Mohan Jee's grandson, Sundar Jee had a conversation with Guru Jee here at Goindval during this visit. Sundar Jee had written a Shabad called 'Sadh' which was authored at Sri Guru Amar Das Jee's passing. Guru Jee agreed to include this Shabad in Gurbani and said if it is read at funerals it will destroy the grief of the deceased.

The Pothia were now respectfully transported from Goindval to Ramdaspur.

16. Meeting Baba Dattu Jee

On route to Ramdaspur Guru Jee and the Sikhs arrived at Khadur Sahib, here the son of Sri Guru Angad Dev Jee, Baba Dattu Jee resided. Upon hearing of Guru Jee's arrival Baba Dattu Jee came and bowed to Guru Jee, Guru Jee stopped him upon his descent to bow to them and spoke humbly praising Baba Dattu Jee. Baba Dattu Jee replied, *"You are the current Guru, it is proper for me to bow to you. I come in faith to you. I made a mistake previously due to which I have pain in my heart and constant pain on my body."*

Baba Dattu Jee narrated how he had kicked Sri Guru Amar Das Jee from their seat when they became the third Guru at Goindval Sahib and on the way back to Khadur Sahib he was robbed by thieves of all the wealth he had looted from Goindval Sahib. In this robbery his foot got injured and he had been in pain ever since and the pain had not gone down at all. He told Guru Jee he had deep regret for the sins he commited and went and met Sri Guru Amar Das Jee just before they passed away and begged for forgiveness. Sri Guru Amar Das Jee had said, *"The fifth Guru will stop the pain that you suffer from."* Baba Dattu Jee now implored Sri Guru Arjan Dev Jee to bless him and abolish the pain in his foot and the constant heart burn he suffered from. Guru Jee looked at him with their glance of grace and dispelled both these pains. Guru Jee stayed one night here too.

The next morning Guru Jee went to meet Baba Dattu Jee and when they arrived, he was in a trance of meditation. When he came out of his meditation he met Guru Jee with much adoration and asked for a boon to become one at the feet of Sri Guru Nanak Dev Jee and then leave his body (pass away) in this spiritual state. Guru Jee granted this boon and left with the Pothia.

17. Compiling Sri Aadh Granth

Guru Jee arrived at Ramdaspur to start the compilation of the anthology that would be revered as 'Sri Aadh Granth' which would later be added to and become 'Sri Guru Granth Sahib Jee' the eternal living embodiment of the Gurus.

First the site to complete the compilation of the Granth was chosen, this is where today stands Gurdwara Ramsar Sahib, Amritsar (about 1km from Harmander Sahib). The site at the time of the compilation was very dense with trees and bushes and very scenic. Guru Jee got gardeners to also plant other flowers to add to the scenic nature of the spot. A natural pond used to form here as the ground was at a lower level. Guru Jee got further excavation work done at the site of the pond and created what is now called 'Ramsar' Sarovar which translates to the 'pool of God.' On the edge of the Sarovar a small tent was erected (to scribe the Granth), in front of this a large marquee was placed to store the ink, paper and house storage units used for the compilation works. Bhai Gurdas Jee was made the scribe and lead for the administration of the whole compilation project.

At Harmander Sahib, Baba Buddha Jee led the administration of the Gurdwara Sahib now, whilst Guru Jee concentrated singularly on the compilation of the Granth. Baba Budhha Jee would meet visiting Sikhs and give guidance to anyone with questions or problems.

The compilation started with ordering Gurbani of the first five Guru's. Sri Guru Arjan Dev Jee made the most contribution to the Sri Aadh Granth – he wrote the most hymns out of all the Gurus (about a third of the whole Granth). Writings of Sikhs and Saints of the Bhakti tradition (Hindus) and Sufi Muslims were also collated. The Sri Aadh Granth began with Japji Sahib, the first Sikh prayer authored by Sri Guru Nanak Dev Jee, followed by the Shabads that made up the 'Rehras Sahib' or evening prayer at the time, which was a few Shabads by various Gurus. This was followed by 'Kirtan Sohila' the prayer to be read before one sleeps at night. After this all other Shabads would follow a systematic ordering of 31 Raags (musical measures), in which Gurbani is ordered by author and length of the Shabads. The Granth was completed on 1st August 1604 and the contents pages were then written. There were a total of 974 leaves or a total of 1948 pages, but some pages were left blank at the end of Raags, also this count includes all pages that were bound including the contents. The Granth's pages were actually 12" x 8" which is a portrait page design and quite small in comparison to the modern standardised landscape designs of Sri Guru Granth Sahib Jee which are reverently kept across the globe nowadays. Bhai Banno Jee got the Granth bound and Sri Guru Arjan Dev Jee added their seal to the Granth. Bhai Banno Jee had also made a copy whilst he got the Granth bound but Guru Sahib did not add their seal to that copy. (A more indepth account of the structure and meanings of Sri Guru Granth Sahib Jee will hopefully be provided in a specific book just on that topic).

Guru Jee completed the Granth for the liberation of humanity, so the words of Gurbani would be immortalised. This divine wisdom would be venerated, studied, meditated upon and sung in musical melodies (Raags); inspiring and liberating genereations. The authenticity of Gurbani was ensured by this act, as even at this early stage of Sikhi some unscrupulous authors had started to use the word 'Nanak' in their writings which was a sign of the writing being authored by one of the Sikh Gurus. The Guru's all ended the majority of their Shabad's with the word 'Nanak' as an author – this was specifically the mode of authorship for all Gurbani of Sri Aadh Granth, very few Shabads do not include 'Nanak' in them.

When Sri Aadh Granth was completed there was a jovial atmosphere and celebrations. The people of Ramdaspur were informed by Baba Buddha Jee of the completion and that there would be a celebratory program at Ramsar Sahib the next day. Hearing this announcement Sikhs travelled in and all came to this auspicious occasion with an array of gifts and offerings of garlands of flowers, food and money.

Guru Jee led the service in which Sikhs had their first glimpse of Sri Aadh Granth, with a Sikh in attendance doing Chaur Sahib (waving a whisk over the Granth which signifies royalty). The Sri Aadh Granth was adorned with fancy spreads and garlands of flowers and many fragrances such as sandalwood and saffron were used to create an adorable aroma. Conch shells were played and 'Jaikare' were bellowed out (war cries, said out of happiness). Kirtan was sung on Rababs – the tradition of singing in the specified Raag at the specified time of day was then strictly followed and only string instruments were used to perform Kirtan accompanied by a Tabla or Jauri. The Raags in Sri Aadh Granth specify both musical measures but also moods, thus certain Raags are only supposed to be sung at certain times of the day and/or for specific occasions. In this way the Kirtani has to be very learned and be able to select which Shabads to do Kirtan of and when.

Sri Guru Arjan Dev Jee explained the greatness of Sri Aadh Granth to the congregation that was gathered in the following way, making these points.

- **"This Pothi (Sri Aadh Granth) is the home of the transcendent Lord. Whoever sings the glorious praises of the Lord of the Universe in the company of the Holy, has the perfect knowledge of God." (1226)**

God is realised by the True Guru's Grace

- Upon seeing the Granth one should clasp their hands and humbly bow.
- By listening attentively to the hymns of Sri Aadh Granth one could attain salvation.
- The physical body of the Guru cannot be seen at all places (a human form can only exist in one place at a time) – the Granth is the heart of the Guru and will remain supreme throughout time. Now, many will be able to get sight of the Guru through this Granth wherever they may reside (thus acknowledging copies would be made and present in multiple locations).
- By taking the Granth to your homes and listening to Gurbani being read, you will obtain much peace and happiness.
- Sikhs should make recensions of the Granth and should remain attentive throughout to ensure accuracy.
- No one should add or remove any Gurbani from the Granth – this is only the work of fools.
- This Granth is the image of God, all your desires can be fulfilled by supplicating humbly to it.
- Those that respectfully keep the Granth will obtain all the blessings that God can give.
- Only the best fragrances such as sandalwood and saffron should be used in the vicinity of the Granth.
- The teachings of the Granth will become enshrined in the lives of those who read or listen to it's hymns attentively.
- The Granth will remove obstacles in the world and make your life worthwhile.

God is realised by the True Guru's Grace

- At the end of services you should make Karah Parshad and distribute it in the congregation.
- All your affairs in the world should begin with a supplication to the Granth.
- When one dies, the family of the deceased should arrange a recital of the Granth.
- All your sins can be abolished by reciting the Granth.

At the completion of this celebratory service Sri Guru Arjan Dev Jee called all the leading Sikhs into a discussion with them, to discuss where the Granth should be permanently housed. It was unanimously agreed that Sri Aadh Granth should be the centre of worship at Harmander Sahib.

On the 1st September 1604, a procession from Ramsar Sahib to Harmander Sahib took place in which the Sri Aadh Granth Sahib was respectfully transported. All the leading Sikhs arrived on this day at Ramsar Sahib at about 2am and did Ishnaan in the Ramsar Sarovar and sat under a large tree and started to meditate. After the meditation, Guru Jee ordered Baba Buddha Jee to take the Granth upon his head and lead the procession to Harmander Sahib, Guru Jee did the Chaur Sahib themselves. Conch shells were played and shouts of joy could be heard whilst the procession made its way forward. Sri Hargobind Sahib Jee also accompanied the procession.

Upon arrival at Harmander Sahib, Kirtan was already being sung and the Granth was respectfully placed in the centre of Harmander Sahib upon a Manji Sahib (a small cot like structure). At the end of the Asa Dee Var a 'Hukamnaama' was taken from Sri Aadh Granth. A Hukamnaama is a Shabad taken at random from the Granth, read for guidance – it is seen as the

Guru speaking to the supplicant(s) directly with words of wisdom. Baba Buddha Jee was thus the first 'Granthi' or reader of the Granth, the Hukamnaama he read was,

God has stood up to resolve the affairs of Saints; coming in person to complete their tasks. The land is beautiful (of Ramdaspur), and the pool is beautiful (the Sarovar); within it is contained the Ambrosial Water (Immortal nectar). The Ambrosial Water is filling it, God has helped me complete the task at hand (building Harmander Sahib and the Sarovar); all my desires are fulfilled. Congratulations are pouring in from all over the world; all my sorrows are eliminated. The Vedas and the Puraanas sing the Praises of the Perfect, Unchanging, Imperishable Primal Lord. The exalted creator - God has kept to His innate nature; Nanak thus meditates on His name (in gratitude). ||1|| The Creator has given me the nine treasures, wealth and spiritual powers, and I do not lack anything. Eating, spending and enjoying, I have found peace; the gifts of the Creator Lord continually increase. His gifts increase and shall never be exhausted; I have found the Inner-knower of hearts. Millions of obstacles have all been removed, and grief does not come near me. Tranquillity, peace, poise and bliss prevail in abundance, and all my desires are abolished. Nanak sings the Glorious Praises of his Lord and Master, whose Glorious Greatness is wonderful and amazing. ||2|| It was God's job, and God has done it; what can the mere mortal do? The devotees are adorned, singing the Glorious Praises of the Lord; they proclaim God's eternal victory. Singing the Glorious Praises of the Lord of the Universe, bliss wells up, and we are friends with the Saadh Sangat, the Company of the Holy. He who made the effort to construct this sacred pool (Amritsar) - how can his praises be recounted? The merits of the sixty-eight sacred shrines of pilgrimage, charity, good deeds and immaculate lifestyle, are found in this sacred pool. It is the natural way of the Lord and Master to purify sinners; Nanak takes the Support of the Word of the Shabad. ||3|| The treasure of virtue is my God, the Creator Lord; what Praises of Yours should I sing, O Lord? The prayer of the Saints is, "O Lord and Master, please bless us with the supreme, sublime essence of Your Name." Please, grant us Your Name, grant us this blessing, and do not forget us, even for an instant. Chant the Glorious Praises of the World-Lord, O my tongue; sing them forever, night and day. One who enshrines love for the Naam, the Name of the Lord, his mind and body are drenched with Ambrosial Nectar. Prays Nanak, my desires have been fulfilled; gazing upon the Blessed Vision of the Lord, I live. ||4||7||10|| (Sohee, 783)

This historical event is commonly referred to as the 'Pehla Parkash' which means the first enthronement of Sri Aadh Granth. After reading the Hukamnaama Baba Buddha Jee also read Japji Sahib from the Granth.

At night Baba Buddha Jee asked Guru Jee as to where the Granth should be taken at the end of the service. Guru Jee said, *"The Granth is God in physical form, read Kirtan Sohila and then bring the Granth to my place of rest."* So after reciting Kirtan Sohila the Granth was respectfully taken to Kotha Sahib which used to be where Sri Guru Arjan Dev Jee used to take rest – this is now in Sri Akaal Takhat Sahib (the highest temporal seat of the Sikhs, a Gurdwara opposite Harmander Sahib). The Granth was placed on the bed of Guru Jee for the night and Guru Jee slept on the floor – this was the level of respect given to Gurbani and the Granth, by Guru Jee.

In this way a daily timetable of bringing the Granth to Harmander Sahib during the morning service; after Asa Dee Vaar had started, was begun. The Granth would then be taken to Kotha Sahib at night – much like the daily timetable that takes place nowadays.

18. Engagement of Sri Hargobind Sahib and Chandhu

Chandhu Shah was a minister of the Mughal Emperor Jahangir, his home was in Lahore – he spent most of his time between Delhi and Lahore. He was a Khatri by caste and quite wealthy. Chandhu had a daughter called Sda Kaur, she was 7 years old and her parents thought they should get her engaged.

Due to the Mughal rule a new trend of non-Muslims getting their children married at a very young age had begun. The common way to find a suitable bride/groom was to appoint a Brahmin (high caste Hindu, usually a priest) and a barber (naiee caste) to become matchmakers. This duet of two men would assess suitable candidates based upon their credentials – the Brahmin was seen as wise so he could assess a match in terms of intellectual match and the barber was seen as expert in matching physical appearance and judging character/personality.

Chandhu told the duet to find a wealthy Khatri (warrior caste) groom from a respectable family, this was in about 1604/5 CE. The Brahmin and barber came to Ramdaspur to have sight of Sri Hargobind Sahib as Guru Jee's family met the credentials set of wealth and caste. The two witnessed affluence and much respect and adoration of Guru Jee and their family. Sri Hargobind Sahib was handsome, muscular and illuminatingly wise. The duet told Guru Jee that they had decided that Sri Hargobind Sahib would be the best match for Sda Kaur and that upon arriving at Delhi they will dispatch gifts from Chandhu's family confirming the engagement.

When the barber and Brahmin arrived at Delhi to meet Chandhu, Chandhu broke out into a rage of arrogance and said to the Brahmin, *"Oh priest what have you done? You have tried to join the brick of a mansion with that of an impoverished home! They are saints and I am a Minister- did you not think of anything? But what can I do now? I don't have a second groom to wed her to."* Traditionally you would just accept the final choice of the Brahmin and barber. In this situation Chandu also new that publicly the Sikhs would know of the proposed engagement, thus his honour would be at risk as would that of his daughter if he had no other plan of marriage for her.

These utterances of Chandu – disrespecting the house of the Guru were learnt of by the Sikhs of Delhi and they were outraged at Chandhu's arrogance. These Sikhs wrote a letter to Guru Jee requesting the cancellation of the proposed engagement. Guru Jee accepted the plea of the Sikhs and cancelled the proposed engagement of Sri Hargobind Sahib to Sda Kaur.

19. Sulhi Khan

Chandhu now became an enemy of the Guru as he was not pleased that the engagement to his daughter had been refused. He had been publicly disgraced as news spread about what had happened. Whilst, Prithi Chand also continued with his enmity with Guru Jee.

The areas adjoining Ramdaspur had lowering income from taxes to the Emperor. The populations in these areas on the majority were followers of Guru Jee. Chandu used this as an excuse to send Sulhi Khan with delegated power from the Emperor to go and collect tax returns and also pursue the wealth of the Guru under the guise of gaining taxes.

On the way to Ramdaspur, Sulhi Khan went to discuss the matter with Prithi Chand who was residing at his village Kothe (now called Kotha Guru, Bathinda). The Sikhs of Delhi learnt of Sulhi Khan's visit and plans – they wrote a letter asking Guru Jee to make preparations for his visit, to counter anything untoward occurring. The leading Sikhs and Guru Jee met to discuss the situation, which is reflected in this Shabad in which Guru Jee describes their planning,

Firstly, the Sikhs advised me to send a letter. Secondly, they advised me to send two men (to Delhi). Thirdly, they advised me to make the effort and do something. But I have renounced everything, and I meditate only on You, God (to resolve the matter). (371)

Guru Jee said to the Sikhs who were in anxiety, *"Do not worry, God is our protector. If God wishes Sulhi Khan will not even be able to reach here."*

Whilst at Kothe, Prithi Chand was lavishly serving and entertaining Sulhi Khan. Prithi Chand went to show Sulhi Khan his brick kiln one day when they were both returning from a hunting expedition. Sulhi Khan kicked his horse to go faster and was trying to show off, his horse bolted forward, slipped and fell straight into the brick kiln which was alight. The fire in the kiln was very fierce and Sulhi Khan along with his horse burnt alive, crying in pain and agony. All efforts to save Sulhi Khan were futile and after much effort his body was removed from the fire and buried. When this news was heard at Ramdaspur, Guru Jee uttered the following Shabad,

The Lord saved me from Sulhi Khan. The emperor did not succeed in his plot, and he died in disgrace. ||1||Pause and contemplate (upon this). The Lord and Master raised His axe, and chopped off his head; in an instant, he was reduced to dust. ||1|| Plotting and planning evil, he was destroyed. The One who created him, gave him a push. Of his sons, friends and wealth, nothing remains; he departed, leaving behind all his brothers and relatives. Says Nanak, I am a sacrifice to God, who fulfilled the word of His slave. (825)

20. Humility & Peshawar congregation

Praise of Sri Guru Arjun Dev Jee had spread across Asia and beyond, into countries like Bangladesh, Afghanistan, Tibet and many more. Sikhs are welling up with so much love and faith, as well as a feeling of bairaag (spiritual separation) and are taking long journeys to see their beloved Guru - some coming once every 6 months and others once a year to Amritsar.

They bring with them gifts and donations of food, clothes, money and many more items, all brought with love and devotion. To many Sri Guru Arjun Dev Jee seems like an 'ordinary man' as they have kept their spiritual capability hidden, with a robe of humility.

Some blessed Sikhs who travelled for many days to see their Guru from Peshawar (some accounts say they were from Kabul), stopped for a rest a few miles away from Amritsar. It was their first visit to have the blessed company of the fifth Guru. When they stopped to take rest, they had all their needs taken care of by a very kind Sikh man who massaged their tired legs and feet, who left them after serving them.

When these Sikhs reached Amritsar and asked where the Guru was, a wise elderly Sikh pointed to that same 'Sikh man' who had come the night before and served them. They ran and fell at the feet of Guru Sahib and begged for forgiveness, for they didn't know he was the Guru. They were amazed by the humility of Guru Sahib who had come and served them, showing he knew his beloved Sikhs were tired on their travels to meet him. The Sikhs shed tears of gratitude and were in bliss, falling at the feet of the Guru.

21. Plotting of Prithi Chand & Chandu

As the praises of the fifth Guru increase tenfold, Sri Guru Arjun Dev Jee's eldest brother Prithi Chand was burning with envy and anxiety. Prithi Chand had wanted to become the Guru after his father Sri Guru Ram Das Jee but the glory could only be Sri Guru Arjan Dev Jee's as he was the one blessed with spiritual enlightenment.

Seeing the state of her husband Prithi Chand, Karmo, his wife turned to him and convinced him to not let anxiety get the best of him. She advised him that he must write a letter to Chandu Shah, a courtier from emperor Jahangir's court who holds great influence in the Emperor's court and complain about their 'enemy' Sri Guru Arjun Dev Jee.

A follower of Prithi Chand took the letter written and presented it as a letter from 'Guru Prithi Chand' to Chandu. In it Prithi Chand stated that he woke up every morning and prayed for Chandu Shah's wellbeing. (Even today some 'Sikh' leaders also make such claims and prayers for ministers in governments showing their alliances to political power).

Chandu replied by saying he is on Prithi Chand's side to become the Guru of the Sikhs as he is also seething from the refusal from Sri Guru Arjun Dev Jee (as requested by the true Sikhs) for Sri Hargobind Sahib Jee's hand in marriage with Chandu's daughter. Chandu said he will give the Guruship over to Prithi Chand and also all the money and donations that the Sikhs gave to the Guru's house. Chandu was drunk on his own power and ego, through his political post he thought he could achieve these things, little did he know he was just plotting the path to his own demise with such hateful plans.

Chandu was fixed upon a plan to either kill Sri Guru Arjun Dev Jee or force Maharaj's son Sri Hargobind Sahib Jee to marry Chandu's daughter, he confirmed this in a letter to Prithi Chand. Both Prithi Chand and his wife Karmo are ecstatic at this response.

Chandu thought of a plan of attack and convinced Jahangir that in India's hottest months, the Emperor should enjoy the cool breeze, scenery and different fruits and vegetation of Kashmir, rather than stay in the heat of Delhi. Jahangir, believing Chandu was speaking in his best interests, praised Chandu and left Delhi with his wives and half of his army for Kashmir.

On route to Kashmir, the Emperor along with his entourage set up camp in Doaba in Punjab and he decided to go for a hunt with a few trusted army personnel. During the hunt the Emperor fell off his horse and injured his leg badly. When he got to the camp, all Jahangir's employees were pained at the sight of his leg and immediately sought medical assistance.

Confused at the cause of his deep wound, the Emperor asked Chandu to bring his astrologer and explain why he got injured. Chandu seized the opportunity and stated that the Emperor's astrologer had been kidnapped and other personal possessions and money had been stolen by some of the many thieves in the area. Shocked, Jahangir enquired who the thieves were, who dared to steal from him. Chandu replied, *"Arjun Dev, the one posing as the fifth Guru, after Nanak. He runs a network of thieves and has no fear of the Empire."*

God is realised by the True Guru's Grace

In utter disbelief, the Emperor asked Chandu if he had lost his mind to suggest such a thing. Jahangir went on to remind Chandu about the Great Guru Nanak, who his forefather Babbar had the good fortune to meet. Chandu still persisted and claimed that Sri Guru Arjun Dev Jee is not the same as Guru Nanak and slanders Guru Jee gravely, calling them a scheming liar and thief. Again, Jahangir remembered the compassionate third Guru, Sri Guru Amar Das Jee, who was gifted with 84 villages by Emperor Akbar when he gained a fort in battle due to Sri Guru Amar Das Jee's boon.

During this conversation, just with Jahangir speaking of the first and third Guru with respect and faith, the Emperor's leg mysteriously healed. The creative force of God had shown the power of singing the praises of the Guru's in this miracle of healing.

***

God shows his power to us but we need to be receptive to it and acknowledge it too and not just be dismissive. He plays a game of hide and seek in the universe, being mostly invisible to us, but those who seek, do surely find God.

22. Sulbhi Khan

After Chandu's conversation with the Emperor Jahangir regarding his leg injury and missing astrologer, Chandu retired to his room.

During the night, Sulbhi Khan, the nephew of Sulhi Khan entered Chandu's room. Sensing the purpose of Sulbhi Khan's visit, Chandu began to berate him, calling him a coward and asking how his conscience let him sleep at night - as it was Sri Guru Arjun Dev Jee that his uncle Sulhi Khan went to kill, yet he met his own death on the way while displaying his horsemanship in ego and falling into a brick kiln.

Sulbhi Khan had heard the conversation between Chandu and Jahangir and stated that this was the opportunity he was waiting for, to avenge his uncle's death. He said his aunt's (Sulhi Khan's wife) tears and taunts kept pushing him to put an end to the Guru, even if he had to resort to the use of black magic.

The mountainous egos of both Chandu and Sulbhi Khan collectively constructed a plan of action - it was decided that in the morning during Jahangir's court, Chandu would bring up the issue of the Emperor's missing possessions and at the same time Sulbhi Khan would announce that another robbery had taken place last night. At this moment Chandu would suggest Sulbhi Khan as a suitable person to send to Amritsar to meet Sri Guru Arjun Dev Jee and investigate the robberies.

Sulbhi Khan boasted privately to Chandu that he would imprison Guru Sahib and during nightfall, behead him. Both evil men agreed that the Emperor must not know of their plan as he still held good wishes towards the Guru.

In the morning, as per their plan, everything fell into place and the Emperor agreed to send Sulbhi Khan, but insisted he went humbly and made a request before Guru Jee that it is improper to house thieves. With good intentions, Jahangir also told Sulbhi Khan to ask Sri Guru Arjun Dev Jee the reason for engaging in such acts and if there is a financial shortfall in the Guru's House or from the 84 villages (which were gifted to the third Guru in Emperor Akbar's time), then the Royal Treasury will happily make up the shortfall.

At the behest of his courtier Chandu, Jahangir sent Sulbhi Khan to Amritsar to investigate the theft and relocate the Emperor's missing possessions. Sulbhi Khan happily responded by saying he will find out everything, even if he has to bribe the locals for information. He goes on further stating that if he finds Sri Guru Arjun Dev Jee or their Sikhs committed the theft, then he will decide how to gain justice by either imprisoning or killing them. Sulbhi Khan boasted that by shaking a tree one is bound to gain fruit and this is what he intended to do to Guru Sahib. After saying this, he left the Emperor's camp.

The author Bhai Santokh Singh Jee (1768 – 1832 CE) explained that this foolish person (Sulbhi Khan) didn't understand that only death would be his fruit (reward) coming off the tree that he would shake. For no reason he is picking a fight with Sri Guru Arjun Dev Jee, just like his uncle Sulhi Khan had.

Whoever has enmity with that being who is without enmity (nirvair), only reaps the worst death and when he cries and is dragged into the horrid hells, no one will be his support.

Sulbhi Khan left with a small force of men imagining his glorified conversations with his relatives after doing the deed which he is set upon committing. Meanwhile, Jahangir and Chandu Shah leave for Lahore and Chandu built his hopes for revenge and anticipated Sulbhi Khan's good news.

When Sulbhi Khan arrived 30 miles away from Amritsar (the residence of Sri Guru Arjan Dev Jee) he and his men crossed paths with a Muslim soldier known as Sayed Khan and his small band of men. After greeting each other, Sayed Khan asked where Sulbhi Khan is travelling to. Sulbhi Khan replied that he is on a mission for the Emperor, heading to Amritsar.

Sayed Khan stated that he along with his soldiers had come to meet with him with an important concern, *"We are employees of your uncle Sulhi Khan. We've worked for a whole year for your uncle but not received any wages. As you are the next of kin, you need to pay us what we are owed and keep your family's name untarnished."*

Sulbhi Khan had no knowledge of any money owed and asked Sayed Khan to meet him in Lahore to discuss the money owed with Chandu. The two exchanged heated words and Sayed Khan told Sulbhi Khan it is now or never and blocked Sulbhi Khan's path to leave.

Upon seeing his path obstructed Sulbhi Khan was enraged and swears loudly at Sayed Khan. Sayed Khan pulled his punchdagger out and stabbed Sulbhi Khan in his stomach. The person who thought he could kill that perfect, powerful and compassionate Guru, fell to the ground with his stomach ripped open, bleeding to death. Just as Chandu was awaiting Sulbhi Khan's good news of revenge, Sulbhi Khan's soldiers appear and reported Sulbhi's death.

After a few days the Emperor called Chandu and asked the whereabouts of his man, Sulbhi Khan. A depressed Chandu relayed the events of Sulbhi's death, Jahangir reprimanded Chandu, calling him a liar and foolish, saying Guru Sahib is highly respected and powerful. Chandu was left speechless and bewildered, as to how two of his allies had died on their mission and failed to understand that this great Guru was beyond fear.

23. Prithi Chand leaves for Lahore

Chandu, after hearing the Emperor Jahangir's response to Sulbhi Khans death, returned home and received a letter from Prithi Chand. In the letter, Prithi Chand, enquired as to what is to be done now, in terms of destroying the fifth Guru, as so far all attempts have failed. He suggested to Chandu that he should be called to Lahore to meet the Emperor in person and gain his assistance on the matter.

Whilst Jahangir is still addressing Sri Guru Arjun Dev Jee with respect and he refused to trouble Guru Sahib, but agreed to meet with Prithi Chand. Chandu sent a messenger to Prithi Chand with an invitation from the Emperor to meet him in Lahore.

Karmo, Prithi Chand's wife had grave concerns about the future wellbeing of her husband and tried her best to prevent him from going to Lahore, even stating that this enmity with Sri Guru Arjun Dev Jee should be forgotten. However, Prithi Chand pays no heed to Karmo's intuition and left for Lahore, wishing goodbye to his family and friends.

As Prithi Chand and his followers pass Tarn Taran Sahib Gurdwara (also known as Darbar Sahib), his followers made a request to Prithi Chand that they desired to bathe in the Sarovar (water tank constructed by Sri Guru Arjan Dev Jee) and rest there and then move on the following day. Prithi Chand responded angrily and slandered the Sarovar in the following way, *"This is not a place of pilgrimage - it's a swamp full of rubbish."* He further claimed that he built Sri Harmandir Sahib and will prove this to his followers by also visiting there.

Unable to keep his word, Prithi Chand did not visit Sri Harmandir Sahib and took his companions to his father-in-law's village Heri instead and called this village a place of pilgrimage. Prithi Chand and his followers spent some days resting, enjoying food and informing the villagers of how he is the 'True Guru.'

On the third night Prithi Chand told everyone that they will leave for Lahore in the morning. A few hours after the evening meal which Prithi Chand ate a great deal of, Prithi Chand woke up crying in pain, screaming, that he is dying in pain – the food he ate had been contaminated with Cholera. Realizing he could not survive, Prithi Chand asked for his last rites to be held at Heri and sent a message to his son Mehrbaan to never forget to claim the Guruship and murder Sri Guru Arjun Dev Jee.

24. Jahangir invites Guru Jee to his court

Karmo (Prithi Chand's wife), fearing the fate which her son Mehrbaan may also face, if he took on his father's last dying request about keeping enmity with Sri Guru Arjun Dev Jee, told Mehrbaan the great history of all the Gurus and successfully halted him from meeting with Jahangir.

Meanwhile, Chandu heard about Prithi Chand's demise and felt highly anxious about what action to take next. Chandu's was desperate to fulfil his desire and take revenge on Guru Sahib for refusing his daughter's hand in marriage, for their son, Sri HarGobind Sahib. Chandu's own failed attempts at payback were causing him great physical and mental stress.

Chandu once again tried to manipulate the Emperor Jahangir by talking sweetly of Jahangir's forefathers and how they were always shown respect. Chandu told Jahangir about the 'real' Guru Prithi Chand passing away and how he was the rightful heir to become the Guru of the Sikhs. Chandu praised Prithi Chand for being full of great qualities such as contentment, faith and truth and continued commenting that Sri Guru Arjun Dev Jee was very egotistical and had never shown respect to Jahangir by visiting him, whereas Prithi Chand would have happily come and bowed to the Emperor.

Chandu convinced Jahangir to send a Siropa (robe of honour) to Mehrbaan which Jahangir then gave to Chandu to send to Mehrbaan, along with a message stating that Mehrbaan should stay in his village and consider himself the next Guru. Chandu slandered Sri Guru Arjun Dev Jee to Jahangir by claiming that Guru Sahib viciously threw Prithi Chand out of Amritsar and was now sending their Sikhs far and wide to steal money to construct Sri Harmandir Sahib and accumulate more wealth.

The Emperor recognised Sri Guru Arjun Dev Jee's divine power and refused to believe Sri Guru Arjun Dev Jee was a thief, but for Chandu's argument sake he agrees to call Sri Guru Arjun Dev Jee to his court, for the truth to be revealed. Delighted at the Emperor's cooperation, Chandu started to plot again, thinking of how he could kill Sri Guru Arjun Dev Jee Maharaj.

25. Baba Sri Chand & Bhai Kamaliye

Baba Sri Chand was the eldest son of Sri Guru Nanak Dev Jee and was still alive during the times of the fifth Guru. Every year the Gurus would send 500 rupees to Baba Sri Chand out of respect and to keep his Dera (abode, where Udaasis originated from) going.

One day Baba Sri Chand called his close servant Bhai Kamaliye and ordered him to go to Amritsar to Sri Guru Arjun Dev Jee and request his annual 500 Rupees, along with an extra 500 Rupees and a horse out of happiness on Sri Hargobind Sahib Jee's wedding. Bhai Kamaliye was told to specifically ask for the gifts in a forceful, stubborn way and not to sit or be content until he received them.

When Bhai Kamaliye got to Amritsar he made the request to Sri Guru Arjun Dev Jee who happily obliged and sent Bhai Kamaliye to have food in the Langar. When Bhai Kamaliye got to the Langar hall he saw countless Sikhs waiting to be served by Sri Guru Arjun Dev Jee's wife, Mata Ganga Jee.

Impatiently Bhai Kamaliye called out for Langar whilst still standing up, and after the second time he made this request, Mata Ganga Jee (who was already rushed) hastily replied, *"Why are you standing like a soldier? Sit down and join the rest of the congregation and you will be served."*

Mata Ganga Jee served Bhai Kamaliye as soon as she could and even then, remembering his strict orders not to sit down, Bhai Kamaliye ate his food standing up. After eating, Bhai Kamaliye rushed back to Sri Guru

Arjun Dev Jee's side and stood in front stating that he would not leave until Guru Sahib granted those gifts.

Guru Jee presented Bhai Kamaliye with the gifts along with a Sikh to help take the gifts back to Baba Sri Chand. Back at the dera, Baba Sri Chand was happy with the gifts and asked Bhai Kamaliye to relay everything that happened when he requested these gifts impatiently. Baba Jee asked if Guru Jee was angry, stressed, or cool and collected. Bhai Kamaliye replied that Sri Guru Arjun Dev Jee was just as calm and graceful after the request, as they were before he made the request. When Bhai Kamaliye told Baba Sri Chand about the words Mata Ganga Jee spoke to him while waiting for Langar, Baba Jee was not impressed and mystically replied, *"If they call hungry people soldiers, then in their house soldiers will come who will speak bitterly and put false charges upon their family."*

After saying these unchangeable words, Baba Sri Chand then counted the money that Bhai Kamaliye brought and found it was the exact amount he requested. On seeing the horse that was also gifted, Baba Jee became pleased and then said these words, *"The stables and horses* [in the Guru's House] *will increase and so will the armies."*

These two predictive statements shocked the Sikh (who had come along with the gifts) who took permission to leave and upon return, he informed Sri Guru Arjun Dev Jee of what had been stated. Mata Ganga Jee was also standing near Sri Guru Arjun Dev Jee when the Sikh narrated what had been said and felt deep regret. Sri Guru Arjun Dev Jee further enquired as to what had happened in the Langar hall and on Mata Jee's response, said that Baba Sri Chand's words will come true as he is a very respect worthy and a spiritually advanced individual. Even after hearing these words (curse and boon), Sri Guru Arjun Dev Jee remained calm and unaffected, living happily in the will of God, letting destiny unfold.

***

26. Meeting Khusro

Khusro was the Emperor's son and for some reason he had been exiled by his father Jahangir. Messages were sent far and wide for nobody to entertain Khusro. This left Khusro with a handful of men and in search of sanctuary.

At this time, Sri Guru Arjun Dev Jee was in Taran Taaran and had been there for some days. Khusro, on reaching Punjab heard the praises of Sri Guru Arjun Dev Jee and developed a desire to meet them. On seeing the grandeur of the Guru's court, the beautiful, lifting kirtan (devotional hymn singing) and the rush of sangat (congregation) waiting for a glimpse of Guru Jee or on hand to serve them, Khusro's mind was lifted.

When Khusro came close to Guru Sahib, he prostrated and paid his humble respects while telling Maharaj of his bleak situation. Sri Guru Arjun Dev Jee, the embodiment of compassion became merciful and granted Khusro with food, shelter, 5000 rupees and other blessings. After a few days Khusro made his way towards the Sindh province.

Chandu received news of this meeting and immediately sought his opportunity to inform the Emperor Jahangir and stir up a storm of anger and infuriation. Chandu continued describing Guru Jee as a rebel of the government, with no fear or respect for Jahangir. He painted a tainted picture of Guru Sahib with his rabid slander and insisted that the Emperor should call Sri Guru Arjun Dev Jee to account for his actions, or a full rebellion would occur (led by Khusro).

27. Message from Jahangir

As per Baba Sri Chand's prediction, a soldier on the command of Jahangir and Chandu was sent to intimidate Sri Guru Arjun Dev Jee and deliver a letter ordering a fine of 200,000 rupees. Although the soldier had set off with specific instructions to disrespect and humiliate the Guru's House, when the soldier arrived in the presence of the True Guru, his heart and mind became illuminated and all his negative thoughts receded.

The soldier became so enraptured by the Guru's grace that he asked for forgiveness for his original intentions and told Maharaj everything about Chandu's evil designs. Sri Guru Arjun Dev Jee blessed the soldier and sent him back to Lahore with a message, that they themselves will come to Jahangir's court. The soldier left Amritsar with a humble request that he may become the Guru's Sikh too.

Chandu added more fuel to the fire, by running to the Emperor and tried his best to expose the Guru's 'audacity' at not fearing the Government and not paying the fine. Jahangir advised Chandu to wait some days for the Guru's arrival.

***

The above accounts of Jahangir's relationship with Sri Guru Arjan Dev Jee are taken from 'Suraj Parkash' by Bhai Santokh Singh Jee. Bhai Vir Singh Jee in his writings does elaborate that historically there is the view that Jahangir had enmity towards the Sikh Guru's and was party to the martyrdom of Sri Guru Arjan Dev Jee. I will now quote directly from the memoirs of Jahangir 'Tuzuki-I-Jahangiri' translated by Alexander Rogers, which clearly demonstrate his personal beliefs. It has been argued that Jahangir privately ordered the death of Guru Sahib but publicly got the blame shifted to Chandu. This is what he writes,

"In Gobindwal, which is on the river Biyah (Beas), there was a Hindu named Arjun, in the garments of sainthood and sanctity, so much so that he had captured many of the simple-hearted of the Hindus, and even of the ignorant and foolish followers of Islam, by his ways and manners, and they had loudly sounded the drum of his holiness. They called him Guru, and from all sides stupid people crowded to worship and manifest complete faith in him. For three or four generations (of spiritual successors) they had kept this shop warm. Many times it occurred to me to put a stop to this vain affair or to bring him into the assembly of the people of Islam.

At last when Khusaru passed along this road this insignificant fellow proposed to wait upon him. Khusaru happened to halt at the place where he was, and he came out and did homage to him. He behaved to Khusaru in certain special ways, and made on his forehead a finger-mark in saffron, which the Hinduwan (Hindus) call qashqa (tika) and is considered propitious. When this came to my ears and I clearly understood his folly, I ordered them to produce him and handed over his houses, dwelling places and children to Murtaza Khan and having confiscated his property commanded that he should be put to death."

No other historical accounts that I have read mention the confiscation of property belonging to Guru Sahib but as in any empire, what is reported and what actually happens on the 'ground' can be two very different realities so the memoirs must be read within this spirit of what the emperor ordered. Also, not to discount the role of Chandu, he may have had a major role in misinformation and assisting the decision to ensure the murder and torture of Guru Sahib with full complicity of Jahangir.

One has to also remember that Sri Guru Hargobind Sahib Jee struck friendship with Jahangir later on and historians paint the picture that Jahangir was mininformed by Chandhu and Chandhu was the main instigator and culprit of the Gurus martyrdom. Chandhu was then handed over to Sri Guru Hargobind and the Sikhs to do as they wished, some time after Sri Guru Arjan Dev Jee's Shaheedi. He was eventually beaten to death as punishment from the Sikhs.

***

28. Gurgaddi of Sri Guru HarGobind Sahib Jee

Sri HarGobind Sahib Jee was forever under the tutelage of Sri Guru Arjan Dev Jee and the company of great Sikhs such as Baba Buddha Jee and Bhai Gurdas Jee. He was the natural heir to become the next Sikh Guru. Some teachings imparted to Sri HarGobind Sahib Jee, will now be elaborated.

Sri Guru Arjun Dev Jee, had his ten year old son Sri Hargobind Sahib Jee on his laps and gave him this advice as a perfect father and Guru would, *"We will get happiness by providing the Sangat (congregation) with happiness. Respect Gursikhs (Sikhs of the Guru) and always support them. This practice of being a support to Sikhs was started by Sri Guru Nanak Dev Jee. Memorise Gurbani off by heart. Awake at Amrit Vela (before dawn), bathe, then sit in solitude, meditating upon God and focus on virtue. Then listen to Kirtan (hymn singing) and bless the Sangat with your darshan (sight)."*

The time had now come to anoint Sri HarGobind Sahib Jee as the next Guru. Sri Guru Arjun Dev Jee called a special meeting with his most beloved Gursikhs, Baba Buddha Jee, Bhai Gurdas Jee, Bhai Bidhi Chand Jee, Bhai Jetha Jee and Bhai Piraana Jee. Maharaj also called their son Sri Hargobind Sahib Jee in the room and informed the Sikhs gathered that Sri Hargobind Sahib Jee is now ready for the Guruship, as Guru Sahib will be leaving to sacrifice himself.

All the Sikhs present agreed with this choice and also confirmed that Sri Hargobind Sahib Jee, although only 8 or 9 years of age (historically there is debate on the year of birth some say it was June 1595 others says 1596 CE), is such an all-powerful being that as a Guru he will fight against falsehood and tyranny. Sri Guru Arjun Dev Jee then did 'parkarma' (circumambulated) around Sri Guru Hargobind Sahib Jee and bowed to him as the Sixth Guru. The parkarma is done to show respect. This was on 15th May 1605 CE.

The all-knowing, compassionate true Guru explained to Baba Buddha Jee that it is now time for Sri Guru Hargobind Sahib Jee to become the Guru and gave these words of wisdom. All Sikhs are to:

- to recognise the same light in Sri Guru Arjun Dev Jee to be in Sri Guru Hargobind Sahib Jee;

- follow a new warrior spirit that will be instilled by Sri Guru HarGobind Sahib Jee that will protect righteousness.

Sri Guru Arjan Dev Jee then gave Sri Guru Hargobind Sahib these priceless words of guidance:

- recognise that You are the image of God themselves on the inside, but on the outside keep the conduct of a Bhagat/devotional worshipper (that of humility);

- only use 'miracles' (spiritual powers) under two circumstances- to protect your devotees or uphold God's discipline (maryada);

- awake at amritvela (before dawn) and always be amongst the sangat.

Sri Guru Arjun Dev Jee then explained that the rulers of the land have forgotten the path of justice and adopted ways of cruelty and corruption. For this reason, Maharaj said that they must sacrifice themselves in order for a new warrior spirit to take birth.

***

29. Last words of advice to Mata Ganga Jee

That night, after Guru Sahib's evening meal, Sri Guru Arjun Dev Jee's wife, Mata Ganga Jee, returned to Maharaj's side. With loving words, Sri Guru Arjun Dev Jee called their wife to their side with the utmost respect, telling her she is a great woman with high ideals, and informed her of his departure to Lahore.

Guru Sahib told Mata Jee about her son being blessed with the Guruship and not to have any attachment to physical bodies, as they are false and bound to leave (die). Sri Guru Arjun Dev Jee advised Mata Jee that they are about to leave this world and when her time is right to leave the world, she will reunite back with Guru Jee in SachKhand (the realm of Truth/God). Guru Jee continued by telling Mata Jee of the bliss she will receive from her son and grandsons in the meantime.

Astounded at these unexpected words she heard, Mata Jee became anxious and unstable, she begged her husband Lord - Guru Jee, for some more guidance. Unable to bear the separation from Guru Sahib, Mata Jee's sadness knew no bounds. Mata Jee said, *"You are my Strength and because of you I have had the patience and ability to withstand the attacks on our son Sri Guru Hargobind Sahib Jee."*

The all-knowing and perfect Guru, reassured Mata Jee, by saying, *"Sri Guru Nanak Dev Jee is our true support - Sri Guru Hargobind Sahib Jee is their sixth image and will always be the support of all."* Guru Sahib then looked at Mata Jee straight into her eyes and being pleased with her devotion, blessed her with 'Brahmgian' – divine wisdom and unity with God. Mata Ganga Jee's spiritual eyes opened forth and she then realised why it is important for Guru Sahib to sacrifice themself – in order to save all mankind from tyranny.

30. Leaving for Lahore

The next morning, after completing their morning routine, Sri Guru Arjun Dev Jee requested a Palki Sahib (a palanquin to sit upon to travel) and 5 Sikhs – Bhai Bidhi Chand Jee, Bhai Piraana Jee, Bhai Langaha Jee, Bhai Jetha Jee and Bhai Paira Jee – to leave with them. Maharaj Jee lovingly advised all the congregation to stay at Amritsar and keep having darshan of Sri Guru Hargobind Sahib Jee. Sri Guru Arjun Dev Jee then contemplated on all the Gurus before them for some time and then give their final respects at Sri Darbar Sahib.

Scores of Sikhs, including Sri Guru Hargobind Sahib Jee and Baba Buddha Jee followed the fifth Guru, Sri Guru Arjun Dev Jee in their Palki Sahib to the outskirts of the city of Amritsar. Guru Sahib stopped the sangat (congregation) from going any further and gave the gathered Sikhs these final words:

- Always remember the True Guru and all your pains and troubles will disappear;

- Always follow the advice of Baba Buddha Jee who has always profoundly guided the Sikh Sangat.

Sri Guru Arjun Dev Jee then told Sri Guru Hargobind Sahib Jee to show the utmost respect to Baba Buddha Jee for being the eldest Brahmgiani (enlightened being) and the one who had taught them Gurmukhi. On hearing these words, Sri Guru Hargobind Sahib Jee and Baba Buddha Jee fell at Sri Guru Arjun Dev Jee's holy feet. With tears flowing, all the Sikhs bid their final farewell to Guru Sahib and begged them to keep them in their glance of grace.

Sri Guru Arjun Dev Jee sent a Sikh to Goindwal Sahib to send a message to his cousin Bhai Arth Mal (son of Baba Mohri Jee & grandson of Sri Guru Amar Das Jee) to promptly meet them in Lahore. When Bhai Arth Mal received the message, he became concerned and discussed the message with his family questioning the reasons for Guru Jee's visit to Lahore and left promptly the next morning.

In Lahore, a poor but highly devout Sikh called Bhai Suddhu Jee used to pray daily for Sri Guru Arjun Dev Jee to come to his home. On hearing the pangs of love from this devotee's prayer, Sri Guru Arjun Dev Jee along with the five Sikhs who accompanied them (Bhai Bidhi Chand Jee, Bhai Piraana Jee, Bhai Langaha Jee, Bhai Jetha Jee and Bhai Paira Jee), knocked on Bhai Suddhu Jee's door. The inner knower of hearts Sri Guru Arjan Dev Jee, even while walking to his martyrdom still fulfilled his humble Sikh's only desire.

31. Bhai Suddhu Jee

Bhai Suddhu Jee and his wife were poor Sikhs who had prayed daily for Sri Guru Arjun Dev Jee to come to their home and bless them with the opportunity to serve them. When Guru Sahib was making their way to Lahore (to Jahangir's court), Guru Jee fulfilled this request before their martyrdom.

When Bhai Suddhu Jee saw that it was Guru Sahib knocking on his door, he bowed at Maharaj's holy feet and showered praise upon the true Guru for fulfilling his heartfelt desire. Overwhelmed with love, Bhai Suddhu Jee requested Guru Jee to sit on the throne he had made and reserved for them. With great reverence, Bhai Suddhu Jee placed a sheet on the floor for the five Sikhs accompanying Maharaj to be seated upon.

Bhai Suddhu Jee and his wife first washed Guru Jee's feet and then the feet of the five Sikhs accompanying them. Considering this water to be the purest of the pure, Bhai Suddhu Jee and his family drank the water which contained the dust of the Holy and put droplets of the water around his house to purify it.

Whilst Guru Sahib and the Sikhs rested, Bhai Suddhu Jee and his wife cleaned the kitchen and all its utensils thoroughly. Following that, the couple then went and bathed, putting on fresh clean clothes to start cooking. All different types of food, sweet, buttery, salty, chilli and so forth, were served to Guru Jee and their Sikhs. Bhai Suddhu Jee was always ready to offer more food during the meal, ready to replenish their dishes. When Guru Jee and the Sikhs had finished eating, Bhai Suddhu Jee and his wife washed their hands.

Guru Sahib was pleased with the service and devotion of this couple and praised them, but Bhai Suddhu Jee humbly replied, "It is you Guru Jee, who makes one capable of doing anything."

Right at the end after everyone had eaten, Bhai Suddhu Jee and his wife also ate their dinner. It was nightfall and Bhai Suddhu Jee requested Guru Jee and the five Sikhs to take rest. All night long Bhai Suddhu Jee and his wife massaged Guru Sahib's holy feet and fanned them in the summer heat.

All the Sikhs in Lahore found out that Maharaj was residing at Bhai Suddhu Jee's home and arrived there in droves. A day passed with sangat seeking Guru Sahib's blessings and Bhai Suddhu Jee and his wife hospitably served all those who came to their home. After bathing before dawn, Guru Sahib, the Sikhs and Bhai Suddhu Jee's family meditated on God. With true love in their hearts, this devoted couple obtained the highest blessings from Guru Jee and climbed great spiritual heights.

32. Bhai Arth Mal

Bhai Arth Mal Jee (Sri Guru Arjun Dev Jee's cousin) hastily arrived at Bhai Suddhu's house and on seeing Guru Sahib, bowed down. Guru Jee immediately embraced Bhai Arth Mal Jee with love and respect; getting him to sit close by.

Sri Guru Arjun Dev Jee told Bhai Arth Mal Jee the reasons for why they are going to attain martyrdom. Guru Jee explained that the rulers had become enemies with Sri Guru Nanak Dev Jee's house of Sikhi, which holds no enmity towards anyone. Sri Guru Arjun Dev Jee said, *"By killing me, Chandu and his associates will not escape from their sin and therefore this martyrdom will begin an end to their evil rule (saving millions of others from their injustice). Due to this sacrifice, a new warrior spirit will emerge in Sikhi from Sri Guru Hargobind Sahib Jee. Chandu has falsely accused me and my Sikhs of theft and of aiding Jahangir's exiled son Khusro to rebel. Chandu then sent a letter fining me 200,000 rupees for helping Khusro. By sacrificing my body, the truth will be established and all these accusations and lies will fall on Chandu. That person who tries to stop the truth and good virtues will himself suffer in pain."*

Sri Guru Arjun Dev Jee also explained that when his mother Mata Bhani Jee was younger, she did great Seva (selfless servitude) of her father the third Guru, Sri Guru Amar Das Jee. One day while Sri Guru Amar Das Jee was meditating on a special seat, she saw that one of the legs were unsteady and was about to break. Instead of disturbing Sri Guru Amar Das Jee from his meditation, she kept her hand underneath it and stopped the seat from breaking. Sri Guru Amar Das Jee, after some time noticed her bruised and bloody hand. Pleased with her devotional Seva, Guru Jee told her to ask for a boon. At that time, Mata Bhani Jee asked for the Guruship to remain in her family. Sri Guru Amar Das Jee granted her wish, but also advised that there will be great hardships along with this boon. Mata Jee (who was later married to Sri Guru Ram Das Jee, the fourth Guru) was of a very high spiritual state, she knew that the future for the Gurus and their family would be full of hardship and tests (later the ninth Guru, Sri Guru Teg Bahadur Jee also attained martyrdom along with Sri Guru Gobind Singh Jee's four sons and mother) and wanted the Guruship in her house to save others from this pain of hardships.

Bhai Arth Mal Jee's eyes filled up with tears and he praised Sri Guru Arjun Dev Jee for being so great and steadfast in the truth. He stated that Guru Sahib is the one who always helps all selflessly, while those Moghuls and Chandu will definitely reap the pain of the slander they are sowing. Bhai Arth Mal Jee then put his hands together and begged Guru Jee to let him become a martyr instead of Guru Jee. He pleaded with Guru Sahib that all the Sikhs rely on Guru Jee for everything and, in turn Guru Sahib blesses them with liberation.

Sri Guru Arjun Dev Jee told Bhai Arth Mal this was not desired as he only has forty days left of his life too (Bhai Arth Mal does). Guru Jee blessed Bhai Arth Mal with the ability to not waver and instead continually meditate on God. Guru Sahib then informed Bhai Arth Mal Jee that after forty days they will reunite in Sachkhand (the Realm of Truth in the afterlife).

Great, great is that perfect Guru who himself is liberated and liberates countless others!

33. Chandu burns with envy

Sikhs from far and wide made their way to Bhai Suddhu Jee's home to see Sri Guru Arjun Dev Jee and receive their blessed glance of grace, achieving a state of tranquillity by doing so. One day, Guru Sahib decided to go in his Palki towards the River Ravi with their Sikhs. Situated near the river was Chandu's home. As Chandu looked across from his home, he spotted the rush of people and a majestic person in a Palki.

On seeing such a scene, Chandu first thought that maybe it was a very wealthy person, or perhaps someone with great authority. When he enquired from his soldiers to whom this person was, the soldier replied that it was the great Sri Guru Arjun Dev Jee. Chandu burned with jealousy and ego on hearing his enemy's name. Chandu questioned how it was that Guru Sahib was walking around carefree in his city, whilst all day long he worried about how to destroy Guru Jee. He went to the extent of cursing himself for not hurting Guru Sahib earlier and ran to the Emperor Jahangir.

With great anger, Chandu informed Jahangir that Guru Sahib was in their locality, but had not yet come to present himself. Chandu slandered Guru Jee by saying they make people bow down to them and are attaining great wealth thus – however, they have not paid the fine which was demanded from for sheltering Khusro. Chandu pressed further by declaring that if Jahangir did nothing, Guru Sahib would leave Lahore after taking all the subjects' wealth with them (their donations). Chandu insisted that he would deal with the situation and the Emperor would not have to worry about taking any action himself.

Before his appearance in Jahangir's court, Chandu had bribed other ministers to also put pressure on Jahangir and request that Guru Sahib should be punished for their actions. The court officials even went to the extent of suggesting that Jahangir specifically let Chandu deal with Guru Jee and not the Emperor himself. Jahangir, persuaded by his officials, agreed that Guru Sahib should be called to the court immediately on the pretence of a discussion on God and faith.

Within this court was one person called Wazir Khan, who was also a minister. Jahangir ordered Wazir Khan to go to Sri Guru Arjun Dev Jee and present him in the Emperor's court. With great delight, Wazir Khan happily obeyed and hurriedly made his way to Sri Guru Arjun Dev Jee.

34. Wazir Khan the devout

Wazir Khan, an employee from Emperor Jahangir's court was sent to summon Sri Guru Arjun Dev Jee Maharaj to Jahangir's court. When Wazir Khan reached his destination, he placed both hands together with respect and reminded Guru Jee of when he first met Guru Sahib.

The first time Wazir Khan had come to Sri Guru Arjun Dev Jee, he came to say thank you for curing his pain from the disease endema (swelling of the body by excess water), which had been diminished by listening to Guru Sahib's hymn called 'Sukhmani Sahib' from a local Sikh. Wazir Khan also came to ask Maharaj to cure the actual disease completely, as the pain caused by it had been reduced by listening to Sukhmani Sahib but it hadn't completely been cured. Sri Guru Arjun Dev Jee the epitome of humility pointed to Baba Buddha Jee and referred to him as the 'greatest doctor.'

When Wazir Khan approached Baba Buddha Jee and informed him of everything, Baba Jee was stunned and said Guru Sahib is the greatest doctor. He then sent Wazir Khan back to Sri Guru Arjun Dev Jee. As Wazir Khan got to Guru Sahib, he was then again sent back to Baba Buddha Jee. Baba Jee was carrying a basket and doing Seva (carrying debris) when Wazir Khan repeated his request, Baba Jee struck the now empty basket into Wazir Khan's stomach with such force that all the excess water which had accumulated in his stomach came out and he was cured.

Wazir Khan then continued to tell Guru Sahib of the evil plans Chandu had developed by manipulating generals and the other courtiers through bribery. Although Jahangir was getting heavily influenced, a humble request was made to Guru Jee to come to the court with Wazir Khan and bless Jahangir with their holy company. Guru Jee replied that they were already ready and sat in their Palki Sahib along with their five Sikhs (Bhai Langaha Jee, Bhai Piraana Jee, Bhai Paira Jee, Bhia Biddhi Chand Jee and Bhai Jetha Jee) following them. Numerous sangat lined up the route and recited the praises of Guru Jee as they travelled through the streets of Lahore.

God is realised by the True Guru's Grace

35. Guru Jee arrives at Jahangir's Court

In the court an announcement was made by Wazir Khan that, *"God himself Sri Guru Arjun Dev Jee has arrived."* Wazir Khan had arrived prior to Guru Sahib and had a very high throne prepared for them to be seated upon.

Chandu, already furious at the respect which was shown to Guru Jee with the announcement and high throne, burned even more with jealousy and hatred when other guards and courtiers greeted Guru Jee with respect.

On meeting, the first questions Jahangir asked Sri Guru Arjun Dev Jee were:

1. Who is greater Hindus or Muslims?

2. Who will go to Heaven and Hell?

3. Who does God prefer?

4. Which religion speaks the truth and which is false?

Sri Guru Arjun Dev Jee then gave this profound reply which is now a hymn found in Sri Guru Granth Sahib,

"Some call him Ram Ram (Hindus), some call him Khudaa-i (Muslims). Some serve him as Gusaaee (Hindus) others as Allah (Muslims). Hindus call him the doer as 'Kaarn Karn' Muslims call him 'Kareem' (merciful). God showers grace upon all of us (regardless of denomination). Pause and contemplate (upon this). Hindus bathes at places of pilgrimage, Muslims make their pilgrimage to Mecca called the Hajj. Hindus perform 'pooja' their prayers, whilst

Muslims bow whilst praying. Hindus read the Vedas, Muslims read their books (Quran & other texts which they believe in). Muslims wear blue, Hindus prefer white. Some call themselves 'Turk' (Muslims), some call themselves Hindus. Muslims long for paradise in the afterlife, Hindus long to attain the throne of the angel Indra (devta king). Guru Nanak says that person who has recognised the will of God has realised the true nature of God." (885)

Guru Jee then explained that religions keep creating divisions, but God is only one. People of both religions spend their time arguing in ego and lose the game of understanding. The path of Sikhi also shares the same virtues which exist in Hinduism (of devotional worship) and Islam (of One God), but is more focussed and straight forward as there is no question of who is greater and who is not.

Sri Guru Arjun Dev Jee told Jahangir that a Sikh does not question God's will and has the ability to accept their fate and win the game of life by happily reciting God's Name. Finally, a true Sikh rids themselves of attachment to their body (and others').

Sri Guru Arjun Dev Jee stated that anyone from any religion who followed this way of:

1) Living in God's Will;

2) Continuously reciting God's name;

3) Detaching themselves from their body;

Would attain 'BrahmGian' (divine wisdom of God). Guru Sahib said that he had only summarised in the Shabad (Hymn), but those who had good understanding would understand it, but those without a good level of understanding (of God) and intellect would not.

At this point it is said by other scholars (other than Bhai Santokh Singh) that after this, Jahangir made the following requests to Guru Jee too:

1) Jahangir: *"In Sri Aadh Granth Sahib Jee is there praise of Muslims?"*

   Guru Jee replied with the relevant quotes, such as **'A true Muslim has a compassionate heart' (1084)** but Jahangir still couldn't comprehend the message of the Gurus.

2) Jahangir: *"Include my name (Jahangir) and the year of my rule in Sri Aadh Granth Sahib Jee,*

3) *State it is okay for Sikhs to convert to Islam in Sri Aadh Granth Sahib Jee*

4) *Say Hindus are 'kaafirs' (non-believers of God) and will go to hell*

Guru Sahib flatly refused the final three requests and said this could not be done as it is against the ideals and teachings of the Gurus.

God is realised by the True Guru's Grace

36. Guru Jee taken to Chandhu's house

When Guru Jee refused Jahangir's requests and was about to leave, Chandu quickly turned to Jahangir and told him to let him take Guru Jee to his house and punish him. He asked the Emperor to give him the opportunity to teach Guru Sahib a lesson and stated that all his subjects in his kingdom would be happy at his swift justice.

Chandu told Jahangir to go back to Delhi (rather than Chandu's pre-planned trip to Kashmir, which was not needed now as his objective had been fulfilled) and if anyone asked about Guru Sahib's location, to put them off Chandu's tracks. When Jahangir agreed, all the soldiers surrounded Sri Guru Arjun Dev Jee and the five Sikhs and took them to Chandu's house.

When they reached Chandu's gateway, the five Sikhs with Guru Jee were thrown into a room and locked up. Sri Guru Arjun Dev Jee was taken inside and the soldiers were ordered to keep guard of Guru Jee 24 hours a day, whilst remaining fully armed. The arrest and imprisonment was carried out in such a way that Chandu instructed the guards to make sure no Sikhs should find out about Guru Sahib's presence or try to rescue them. Chandu was extremely delighted at his accomplishment and went to sleep happily.

37. The Torture Begins

As per his plan, Chandu told the Emperor that he is needed in Lahore to oversee the administration and would meet Jahangir in a few days in Delhi. The next morning Jahangir made his way back to Delhi and Chandhu saw him off, whilst Sri Guru Arjun Dev Jee and the five Sikhs were still imprisoned in Chandu's house.

When Chandu returned to his home, he immediately marched over to Sri Guru Arjun Dev Jee. Chandu's eyes were seething with anger and his ego which had been bruised with the refusal of his daughter's hand in marriage with Sri Guru HarGobind Sahib Jee had haemorrhaged into a cause of revenge. Chandu began a tirade of words by stating that twice he had sent a message to Guru Jee to accept the marriage proposal and twice Maharaj refused, causing Chandu great anxiety.

Then Chandu accused Sri Guru Arjun Dev Jee of calling him a dog. Chandu threatened Guru Jee by saying that there is still time to accept the marriage proposal, otherwise he would show Guru Sahib who really is a dog - by killing them like one.

The great Sri Guru Arjun Dev Jee replied fearlessly, *"You called the house of Sri Guru Nanak Dev Jee a pit and called your daughter a brick of a mansion (ornamenting it) and claimed that we were too low for you (in status for the marriage). So, you should seek those so-called 'high' (egotistical) people for your daughter and let us stay with the lowly (humble). I still refuse this proposal. As for me calling you a dog, I did not. If you call yourself a dog then so be it - you are a dog. However, if a Sikh has called you a dog, then a Sikh is the same image as me, and therefore, you are a dog."*

Evil Chandu's blood boiled and his eyes were protruding when he heard these firm words. He ordered his soldiers to not allow Sri Guru Arjun Dev Jee to drink water, eat food or even lie down to sleep. Chandu went further and said if Guru Sahib wanted any water, food or sleep, they would have to pay a 100,000 rupees fine for each request to be permitted. Chandu insisted that either Guru Sahib accepted the proposal of marriage for his son or face death.

Sri Guru Arjun Dev Jee sat unwavering in the extreme heat of June and declared they would not eat, sleep or drink. Meanwhile the five Sikhs – Bhai Paira Jee, Bhai Piraana Jee, Bhai Jetha Jee, Bhai Bidhi Chand Jee and Bhai Langaha Jee – were still kept tied up in ropes in a separate room while Maharaj was kept in isolation. Guru Sahib was not even allowed to stand up or conversate. One whole day and night Maharaj sat in one position without food, drink or sleep.

38. Tortured by being Boiled Alive

Sri Guru Arjun Dev Jee, had been missing for over a day. Sikhs from all over Lahore began desperately searching religious places and homes of Sikhs to locate Guru Jee. They concluded that Maharaj had last been seen going to the Emperor Jahangir's court, so the Sikhs asked the employees of Jahangir's court as to where Maharaj had gone. The Sikhs learnt that Guru Sahib and their accompanying five Sikhs were last seen leaving the court with Chandu and his soldiers.

When the Sikhs approached Chandu's home, they heard the voice of one of the five Sikhs who was accompanying Guru Jee. These five Sikhs were tied up in a room near the doorway and were heard reciting the evening prayer Rehras Sahib. The Sikhs recognising the voice of the Sikh reciting the prayer rushed towards the room, but were quickly halted by Chandu's soldiers who ordered them to return to their homes. At the same time, one soldier turned to the Sikh who was reciting the prayer and shouted at him to stop 'barking' and sit in silence.

The Sikhs who had just arrived felt intimidated by the soldiers thus they returned to their homes. Upon their return, these Sikhs informed others of Guru Sahib's imprisonment.

Later on that same night Chandu came to see how Guru Jee had coped without food, drink and sleep. He continued his attempts to intimidate Maharaj by saying how he would kill them if Guru Sahib did not accept the marriage proposal. The evil Chandu declared that he wanted Sri Guru Arjun Dev Jee to feel the burn in his heart that he felt, when they refused the proposal of his daughter.

Chandhu ordered his soldiers to bring a huge cauldron containing water and told them to heat it by lighting firewood under the cauldron. As the water boiled over and over, Chandu continued with his taunts about accepting the proposal or face death. Sri Guru Arjun Dev Jee replied that they are unaffected by such words and would never accept Chandu's terms. They confirmed that Chandu would meet his fate and receive massive punishment for his sins, and only then would Chandu repent for his sins.

On hearing Guru Jee's words, Chandu retorted by saying, *"First you called me a dog, and now you talk of spiritual matters [by saying I will get punished]."* Chandu ordered his soldiers to throw Guru Sahib into the burning cauldron – but the great Sri Guru Arjun Dev Jee got up and walked voluntarily into the boiling hot water.

The five Sikhs, locked in a room, started crying in pain seeing their beloved Guru sitting in a boiling cauldron. Bhai Piraana Jee, unable to bear the unjust torture of such a merciful Guru, used his astral body to appear in front of Sri Guru Arjun Dev Jee. With palms pressed together, Bhai Piraana Jee, infuriated at the grave sins being committed against Guru Sahib, begged Sri Guru Arjun Dev Jee for permission to destroy Chandu by picking up the cities of Lahore and Delhi in each hand and annihilating them with his spiritual powers.

Just then, one soldier heard those words come from Bhai Piraana Jee's physical body which was still tied up in the room and instantly struck his physical body with a heavy weapon. Guru Jee, seeing his beloved devotee get hit, quickly requested him not to come any closer. Guru Sahib told Bhai Piraana Jee that by accepting martyrdom, they are pulling the roots out of the evil-doers and are not feeling any pain.

Bhai Piraana Jee was such a great Sikh with advanced spirituality, but he still could not tolerate seeing the abuse towards his beloved great compassionate Guru. He begged Guru Jee again for permission to destroy Chandu and Jahangir.

Sri Guru Arjun Dev Jee then reminded Bhai Piraana Jee of where he received these spiritual powers (by doing seva of Guru Sahib) - and that he should not have even an ounce of ego about having them at his beck and call. Guru Jee told Bhai Piraana Jee to sit down and peacefully watch fate unfold, or all the spiritual powers which were gifted to him by Guru Jee, would also be taken back. Guru Jee advised Bhai Piraana Jee to always live in the will of God.

For many hours Sri Guru Arjun Dev Jee sat in the boiling hot cauldron of water, calm and focussed, meditating on God. Even the angel of fire (devta) seeing huge blisters developing on Maharaj's skin, could not bear seeing such a torture on Guru Jee, and changed his innate burning nature from one that burns to one that cools. Thus the cauldron lost its heat.

Chandu, realising much time had passed and Guru Sahib was not going to conform, told the soldiers to take them out of the boiling water and went back to his home for the night.

39. Chandu's devout Daughter-in-Law

The news of Sri Guru Arjun Dev Jee being held captive and tortured, spread throughout Chandu's household. Chandu's daughter in law was originally from a devout Sikh family, before being married to his son Karam Chand. When she found out about Chandu's actions, she was in shock and remembered her parents who always received peace and pleasure from seeing Guru Sahib and meditating on God.

She started contemplating her destiny of being born in a Sikh family, yet having to be married into a family inflicting pain and sin on Guru Sahib. She decided to take food and drink to Guru Jee. She regretted that she would meet Guru Jee under these circumstances and with a heavy heart made her way towards where Guru Sahib is being held captive. She saw a soldier guarding Guru Jee, she became scared, but then offered the soldier a bribe of her jewellery in exchange for some confidential time with Sri Guru Arjun Dev Jee. The soldier agreed and Chandu's daughter in law bowed before Guru Jee, tears streamed down her face when she saw Guru Sahib's blistered body. With her hands pressed together, Chandu's daughter-in-law placed the food and drink before Guru Jee and requested them to eat and drink.

Crying and overwhelmed with love for Guru Jee she was distraught. She could not comprehend the pain her family had inflicted on Maharaj. She expressed sorrow for her past actions (karma) that have caused her to be married into such a sinful household, whereas if she had known this was to happen, she would never have accepted a marriage proposal in this household.

She started begging for forgiveness and asked Sri Guru Arjun Dev Jee to save her from the weight of such sins. Pleased on hearing her request, Guru Sahib referred to her as their daughter and congratulated her for keeping her love for Sri Guru Nanak Dev Jee's house (Sikhi) intact. Maharaj then told her that if she wanted to be saved, she would have to give up her life too, as Maharaj themselves were going to sacrifice their life to uproot the evil-doers.

Guru Sahib explained that eventually Chandu would be brutally punished in this life and the afterlife, and all his dynasty would have to suffer. Sri Guru Arjun Dev Jee also refused the food and water she had bought, as it was from the home of such an evil person. Chandu's daughter-in-law accepted Sri Guru Arjun Dev Jee's advice and agreed to give up her life, humbly requesting Guru Sahib to take her to Sachkhand (realm of truth in the afterlife) with them when they leave their body. At the end of the meeting, Chandu's daughter-in-law returned home depressed. She felt helpless as she knew she could not change fate and stop the evil being orchestrated by Chandu upon Guru Jee.

The next morning, as Chandu ate his breakfast, he reflected upon the fearlessness of Guru Sahib and the lack of pain Guru Jee felt, whilst being tortured. Chandu thought that the water must not have been hot enough. He decided to now heat up sand and torture Guru Sahib by pouring hot sand over them. Thinking such evil thoughts, Chandu first entered the room where the five Sikhs were imprisoned and bounded. He remembered what was said the day before when Bhai Piraana Jee requested Guru Sahib for permission to kill Chandu. Enraged with the lack of fear shown towards him, Chandu boasted that he will not only murder Guru Sahib, but the Sikhs also. After swearing and insulting the Sikhs, Chandu ordered his soldiers to beat these five great God-loving Sikhs mercilessly. All the five Sikhs stayed in the will of the True Guru and took the blows upon their bodies.

Afterwards, Chandu made his way to Guru Jee and started to swear at them, threatening them with more torture, if Maharaj did not accept his daughter's marriage proposal. Chandu psychotically boasted that if Guru Sahib was to refuse the proposal, he would first kill Guru Jee, then his son, wife and the whole family.

In the extremely hot summer month of June, the great Sri Guru Arjun Dev Jee did not eat, drink or sleep in over two days. Their beloved Sikhs were physically beaten and Guru Jee was boiled alive for a whole day. Now Chandu is heating up the sand to further torture Maharaj.

40. Tortured with burning hot sand

The evil Chandu was not satisfied with just depriving Sri Guru Arjun Dev Jee from food, drink and sleep for over two days and torturing Guru Sahib by having them sit in a cauldron full of boiling water. His sadistic mind now decided that he would heat up sand to its highest temperature possible and make Guru Sahib stand on it barefoot, in the scorching hot summer sun. The climate was already unbearably hot, but now with the sand being heated up as well even the skin on Chandu's soldiers is being burnt, whilst they stand around the kiln to heat the sand.

Upon seeing the sand turn white hot, Chandu cruelly boasts loudly to Guru Sahib *"Now I have opened up the doors to hell!"* Turning to his soldiers, Chandu instructed them to them to drag Sri Guru Arjun Dev Jee towards the sand and if Guru Jee showed any hesitation, then the soldiers should beat them until they get onto the sand.

Just as Chandu was in the midst of giving his instructions to his soldiers to drag Guru Jee out of the house, the peaceful Sri Guru Arjun Dev Jee walked out calmly and strode towards the burning sand voluntarily. Sri Guru Arjun Dev Jee is unaffected by their predicament and is teaching us how to be tolerant to pain and have steadfastness like the earth. The earth bears blows when something falls upon it - it is dug up in many ways, and the earth is drowned and burnt at times, but still it never gives up its nature of giving back fruit and vegetation. However, Guru Sahib had gone much further than the earth, in bearing the torture upon their body. Just a few days ago, thousands of people, the faithful, were bowing at the lotus feet of Guru Jee and offering gifts. Yet, today that same Guru is being tortured and abused horrifically, but still shows no sign of discontentment. The sign of a person is how they react in adversity, but the tranquil, immovable, indomitable nature of Sri Guru Arjan Dev Jee is still fully intact.

The stone hearted Chandu insulted Guru Sahib repeatedly claiming that now Guru Sahib's body would burn, just like Chandu's heart burnt when his daughter's marriage proposal was refused. He continued with his bitter words taunting Maharaj by saying at Harmandir Sahib Guru Jee would preach about spiritual matters, but now they have fallen silent.

As Guru Sahib lifted their lotus foot to step onto the sand, they turned to Chandu and said *"Listen, you foolish person, you speak without thinking of the circumstances – you will reap the fruit of your own actions and when I step onto this sand, the roots of your dynasty will be destroyed and you will have to suffer terribly here and in hell (in the afterlife)."*

The greatest of the great, Sri Guru Arjun Dev Jee stepped confidently onto the burning hot sand, but his beloved Sikhs who could see this happening cried out for Maharaj to not continue. Bhai Langaha Jee and Bhai Piraana Jee, cried out to Guru Jee, pleading to Maharaj to let them use their own bodies to lie down on the sand and for Guru Jee to step onto their chests instead. Begging Maharaj that they are unable to see such torture of their perfect Guru, the Sikhs told Maharaj that they are happy to die serving Maharaj, rather than see such injustice.

Great is the Guru who is staying in God's will to take the brunt of the torture upon his body. Great are his beloved Sikhs who are happy to be tortured and die for their Guru. Forever being watchful, the Guru is obedient to God's will and the Sikhs forever in servitude of their Guru are willing to undergo whatever it takes to serve their Guru. The bounds of faith, love and steadfastness are all being heralded for the world in the making of this history of the first Sikh Martyr – Sri Guru Arjan Dev Jee.

When Chandu and the soldiers heard the appeals of the Sikhs to Guru Jee, the soldiers beat them with heavy wooden sticks until they stepped back. The compassionate Guru, seeing their Sikhs assaulted in this way, told them to sit down and accept the will of God. The Sikhs repeatedly expressed their desire to die instead of Guru Jee, but Sri Guru Arjun Dev Jee refused.

Sitting down on the hot sand, Sri Guru Arjun Dev Jee showed no sign of pain or anxiety. In complete equipoise they continued to meditate on God. Seeing this, Chandu told his soldiers to fill ladles with sand and pour the burning hot sand over Guru Sahib's head, back and shoulders. Huge blisters started to appear all over Guru Jee's body. The soldiers continued to torture Sri Guru Arjun Dev Sahib Jee in this horrific manner for six hours but the extraordinary Guru did not even flinch whilst undergoing this cruel inhumane torture.

Guru Jee knows how to tolerate even the most intolerable pain. They are showing all humanity how to bear the most extreme pain with their torture. They exemplify how to be detached from the body and live content by remaining in the will of God. All of the prophets, saints and angels from the nether world watched such a scene unfold in front of their eyes. They all bowed down and exclaimed: *"Great is Sri Guru Arjun Dev Jee! Great is Sri Guru Arjun Dev Jee!"*

41. Saints seek permission to intervene

When night fell all the spiritually powerful beings came to meet the true Guru. They were horrified at witnessing the torture of Maharaj – these spiritualists through their spiritual prowess could see the events unfolding from their respective abodes.

First Gorakh Nath the head of the Yogis/Siddhs came with his followers to Sri Guru Arjan Dev Jee. With his spiritual powers Gorakh Nath put all the soldiers guarding Guru Sahib to sleep. Gorakh Nath paid his respects to Guru Jee and praised Guru Sahib for being completely unwavering through so much torture. He said even though they are all-powerful themselves and capable of destroying the whole universe, let alone Chandu, he wanted to make a humble request. Gorakh Nath requested Guru Jee to allow him to destroy Chandu with his spiritual powers so that no other saint or spiritual person could be hurt by the egomaniac Chandu again.

Sri Guru Arjun Dev Jee replied to Gorakh Nath request by stating that, *"No spiritual person should be scared of anything, even their own death. So being without fear and enmity as is God."* They told Gorakh Nath to also live in the will of God and not interfere in destiny. Hearing Guru Sahib's decision, Gorakh Nath and his followers were left overwhelmed with Guru Sahib's discipline of living in the will of God. They then departed after paying their respects to Guru Jee.

Next, Mian Mir a Sufi saint came to see Guru Jee accompanied by his followers. At a previous meeting, Mian Mir had asked Sri Guru Arjun Dev Jee about a level of spirituality written in Sukhmani Sahib where Maharaj talked about being 'jeevan mukht' – liberated whilst being alive. At that time, Guru Sahib said there will come a time when you will understand what it means.

Mian Mir bowed down to Sri Guru Arjun Dev Jee and asked for a signal to grant permission for him to destroy Chandu. Guru Jee respectfully asked Mian Mir how he perceived differences in the creation, between – a woman, a man, earth, sky, friend, or foes. Guru Sahib explained that there is nothing but one God permeating the whole creation, universality. Maharaj urged Mian Mir to stop seeing differences and understand that there were many reasons why Guru Jee themselves had to sacrifice their body.

Although, some of the reasons for this sacrifice were to bring warrior-spirit into the Sikh faith and to uproot evil doers, it was also to teach those who were already spiritually high to live in the will of God. To teach them to shed their attachments to their bodies and their spiritual capabilities, and to teach them to see the one God at all times. Mian Mir paid his respects and left, saying *"You are great Sri Guru Arjun Dev Jee – you are great."* At that moment the soldiers woke up.

42. Tortured on a hot metal plate

In the morning the cruel Chandu recalled all the torture he had inflicted and reflected upon the fact that it still had not broken the spirit of Guru Jee. The evil, sadistic Chandu, then thought of torturing Sri Guru Arjun Dev Jee by making them sit on a burning hot iron plate (a tavvi). Chandu did just that.

Chandu ordered his soldiers to bring the metal plate (which is usually used to cook chappatis en masse) and heat it to such an extent that the black iron plate turned into the colour of copper. Before Chandu could even instruct his soldiers to bring Guru Sahib, Maharaj came out voluntarily. Guru Jee was ready to embrace their martyrdom. The people who brought the hot plate from the village were chandals. Chandals traditionally did any work which was seen as inhumane or lowly, so they were also undertakers or looked after dead bodies too and were seen as stone-hearted. When the chandals realised what the hot plate was going to be used for they started crying and wailing, calling Chandu a butcher and without even an iota of compassion.

Sri Guru Arjun Dev Jee then stepped onto the hot plate voluntarily they complied at each point of the torture. The helpless five Sikhs who were locked away were in great despair seeing their beloved Guru facing yet another torture. The lotus feet of Sri Guru Arjun Dev Jee became burnt and their pure body was already full of huge blisters from the torture of yesterday. Yet, the evil Chandu laughed and ordered the soldiers to burn more firewood to make the flames of the fire under the hot plate even stronger.

Guru Jee endured this torture peacefully and even though their physical body was slowly disintegrating from the inhumane tortures being inflicted upon it, their spirit was still firm and unshaken.

Guru Jee was teaching us the extremes of patience and peace. Only if one has this peace, can they undergo such torture and voluntarily abide by the orders of torture. Guru Jee set the gold standard for future generations to come.

43. Fifth day of captivity

On the morning of the fifth day of torture, the evil Chandu, with a heart full of anger, approached Sri Guru Arjun Dev Jee Maharaj. The wicked Chandu continued in his attempts to patronise Maharaj by claiming he was the most important courtier within the Mughal Empire and that he had the ear of the Emperor Jahangir. Chandu threatened Guru Jee repeatedly by remarking how Guru Sahib 'didn't know who he was messing with.' He boasted of his newest plans of torture by having Guru Sahib sewn into a bloodied skin of a dead cow and left to suffocate in the burning hot summer sun, as the cattle skin would shrink in the heat.

Chandu's ill-found joy had no bounds when he thought about the deaths of Sulhi Khan, Sulbhi Khan and Prithi Chand. He thought he was great, as it was only him who had gained 'control' over the fate of Sri Guru Arjun Dev Jee. Chandu demanded that if Guru Sahib did not agree to his daughter's marriage proposal, he would not only kill Guru Jee, he would also send his soldiers to Amritsar Sahib to loot the Guru's home and bring the same torture to Sri Guru Hargobind Sahib Jee and the rest of their family.

As a final attempt, Chandu tried his charm and said that it was the last time Guru Jee could ask for something that would be pleasing to Chandu. Chandu even had the audacity to say that if Maharaj accepted the marriage proposal, Chandu would forgive him. The all-knowing Guru, realising Chandu's over-confident ego, intelligently replied that as their body had been extremely burnt over four days, they wanted to go to the river Ravi to bathe and come back fresh to continue this

God is realised by the True Guru's Grace

conversation with Chandu. Maharaj also asked for the five Sikhs to come with them so they too could bathe.

Chandu, believing that Guru Sahib would finally succumb to his threats and agree to his demands, agreed and sent ten armed soldiers to accompany them through a small path to the river, whilst keeping them under contant close surveillance.

Sri Guru Arjun Dev Jee slowly stood up, their whole body was weak and full of blisters. The soles of their feet were completely burnt. Guru Jee wrapped their body with a sheet and took a step forward. Bhai Piraana, one of the five Sikhs ran forward towards Guru Jee. On seeing Bhai Piraana Jee rushing towards them, Guru Jee put their hand onto Bhai Piraana Jee's shoulder and walked on, using them as support for their now fragile body.

As Guru Jee and the five Sikhs made their way through the backstreets to the river Ravi, the local people automatically bowed down seeing Guru Sahib's incredible aura. Even though their body was riddled with blisters and blood, Guru Jee's spirit was unmovable and they were in complete bliss. At the banks of the river Ravi, Guru Sahib reached down and washed their hands and face. Bhai Langaha Jee one of the five Sikhs humbly washed Guru Sahib's lotus feet.

This seva that Bhai Langaha Jee carried out blessed his future lineage. Later on in Bhai Langaha Jee's family would be born his great grand-neice Mai Bhagho who would fight on the front line for the tenth Guru, Sri Guru Gobind Singh Jee. Sardar Baghel Singh Jee was also a descendant of Bhai Langaha, he went on to capture the Red Fort of Delhi in 17833 CE.

Sri Guru Arjun Dev Jee went into the river Ravi and bathed his whole body. When Maharaj came out, they covered themselves with a sheet and sat down on the river bank. Guru Jee then began to recite Japjee Sahib (the first Sikh prayer). The five Sikhs also bathed and returned to Guru Sahib's side to hear the prayer being recited by their beloved Guru. Upon completion of Japjee Sahib, the five Sikhs bowed down at Guru Jee's lotus feet and listened to the final instructions of Sri Guru Arjun Dev Jee.

44. Martyrdom (Shaheedi)

After enduring four days of brutal torture, from being boiled alive in a cauldron, put on burning hot sand and having sand poured all over their head and body and sitting on a burning hot iron plate and not having eaten, drank or slept, Sri Guru Arjun Dev Jee was granted some respite and was allowed to bathe in the river Ravi with his five Gursikhs – Bhai Piraana Jee, Bhai Bidhi Chand Jee, Bhai Langaha Jee, Bhai Jetha Jee and Bhai Paira Jee.

Guru Jee bathed and recited the whole of Japjee Sahib as the five Sikhs respectfully sat beside them. On completion of the prayer, Sri Guru Arjun Dev Jee said these final words of instruction to their beloved Sikhs, *"It is time for me to leave for Sachkhand now. The task that I had been sent here to do is now fulfilled. Meet with Sri Guru Hargobind Sahib Jee and give them confidence that whatever has happened is in the will of God and to accept that will. Tell everyone, including Sri Guru Hargobind Sahib Jee, to not be sad upon hearing news of my torture, but instead sing the praises of God. Sri Guru Hargobind Sahib Jee should bear arms and keep armed forces with them at all times, adhering to all the teachings the previous*

Gurus taught, but now also adding the warrior spirit. Chandu should receive punishment for all of his sins from Sri Guru Hargobind Sahib Jee. The third Guru, Sri Guru Amar Das Jee's family should be called to Amritsar Sahib and along with Baba Buddha Jee, to formally inaugurate Sri Guru Hargobind Sahib Jee as the sixth Guru. When I have left for Sachkhand, do not cremate me - place my body into the river Ravi. My head should be placed on the side where the water flows, and my feet downwards."

At that moment a rababi kirtani (hymn singer who uses a rebeck) came towards Sri Guru Arjun Dev Jee with an instrument in his hands. The kirtani bowed down and Guru Jee asked him to sing shabads (hymns) of separation (bairaag). While the extraordinary emotionally charged kirtan was being sung, many celestial beings arrived at the scene where Sri Guru Arjun Dev Jee was about to relinquish their physical body. Watching from the sky, numerous angels (devi-devte), prophets, spiritual sages, Gorakh Nath and his siddhs, Mian Mir and his followers and many others, all gathered and sung the praises of Sri Guru Arjun Dev Jee. The whole sky was lit up in an unusual spiritual aura.

All the spiritual beings present spoke of Sri Guru Arjun Dev Jee's highest form of truthful living and how they lived in the will of God, teaching patience and steadfastness. *"There is no one else who is like Guru Sahib"*, declared the beings above. With hands folded they awaited Sri Guru Arjun Dev Jee's presence in their abodes.

Sri Guru Arjun Dev Jee lied down on the earth. They took the sheet and covered their whole body and finally drew the sheet over their beautiful face. Sri Guru Arjun Dev Jee left their physical body and entered a chariot to ride to the heavens above, making their way to

Sachkhand. The heavenly drums were sounded, lamps were lit and incense was offered, while white flowers were lovingly thrown over Guru Sahib's head.

Chandu's daughter-in-law, on seeing the sky illuminated in red, realised that Sri Guru Arjun Dev Jee had left their physical body and she fell to the ground herself, discarding her mortal coil (those who are spiritually adept can leave their bodies and die at will). Holding onto Guru Sahib's lotus feet, she also made her way to Sachkhand along with Guru Sahib.

The spiritual beings followed Guru Sahib through the heavens up to where they had access to. Travelling through the realms of Indra and Brahma amongst others, Guru Sahib's praises were sung by the spiritual beings. Sri Guru Arjun Dev Jee eventually reached the highest realm, the realm of truth – Sachkhand and merged back into their primal form, God.

***

Sri Guru Arjan Dev Jee graced the earth for forty-three years, one month and fifteen days. They were the Guru for twenty-four years and nine months. They authored one third of Sri Aadh Granth which would later be added to and become Sri Guru Granth Sahib Jee – the eternal Guru of the Sikhs. They built Harmander Sahib and many more Gurdwaras and sarovars, giving many boons for visiting these Gurdwaras and doing Ishnaan at them. They were the first martyr or Shaheed of the Sikhs and are commonly referred to as the 'crown-jewel of martyrs.'

Guru Jee's greatness cannot be written in words, my ink runs dry. My paper cannot contain Guru Sahib's greatness, for the paper is too insignificant. This book is just a shimmer of light in the life of Sri Guru Arjan Dev Jee whose conflagration is greater than a hundred suns or all the stars we see in the sky. May I and the readers develop an iota of the devotion of Sri Guru Arjan Dev Jee for then our salvation is surely assured.

God is realised by the True Guru's Grace

Glossary

Akhand Paath A continuous reading of Sri Guru Granth Sahiib Jee, usually completed in 48 hours

Baba Respected elder, can also mean paternal grandfather

Bhai Used as a honorific title before ones name. Also literally means brother

Bhatt A bard. The Bhatts wrote Gurbani in praise of the Guru's, which is included in Sri Guru Granth Sahib Jee.

Bikrami A calendar which starts 57 BC and was started by King Vikramaditya, the Sikh Gurus used this calendar.

Brahmgian Knowledge of God

Chaur Sahib Whisk which is reverently swung in the air above Sri Guru Granth Sahib — it signifies royalty/supremacy in the court. In English it sometimes called a 'fly whisk' which it is not, as its function is not to whisk away flies but rather signify leadership of the Granth.

Devta Male angel. Most translate the word to mean diety or God.

God is realised by the True Guru's Grace

Giani	A person who is learned, one of wisdom
Granth	Anthology of prayers
Granthi	Reader of Sri Guru Granth Sahib
Gurbani	Scripture that is either authored by Sikh Guru's and/or accepted as divine verse in Sikh scripture
Gurmukhi	The script created by the Gurus to write Gurbani in. Some argue Gurmukhi is also the language of the Gurus, in that it has its own grammar rules.
Gursikh	A Sikh of the Guru
Gurdwara	Literally means at the 'Guru's door' it is now the common name for the Sikh place of communal worship.
Hukamnaama	A command of the Guru. Sikhs take Hukamnaamas from Sri Guru Granth Sahib Jee by reading a verse by random selection
Jakara	War cry, sounded at the end of services and times of happiness
Jaikare	Plural of Jakara see above
Jee	Used after words to denote respect

Karah Parshad	A sweetmeal made of flour, water, sugar, butter – it is given out at every Sikh service as blessed food.
Kavi	Poet
Kirtan	Devotional hymn singing
Kirtani	One who performs 'Kirtan' (devotional hymn singing)
Langar	The free kitchen in Gurdwaras where meals are served to all visitors for free
Maharaj	Means supreme king, used as an honorific title but also used for monarchs
Manji Sahib	A cot like structure upon which Sri Guru Granth Sahib is seated upon
Mata	Literally means 'mother,' sometimes added as a honorific title before ones name to be more respectful when addressing them or talking about them.
Naam	Translates to 'name' but colloquially in Sikh thought it would refer to Gurbani or the infusion of 'Naam' into a disciple from the Guru when he/she becomes a Sikh in the initiation process

Pothi	Anthology of prayers
Pothia	Plural of 'pothi' see above
Rababi	Rebeck player
Sahib	Means 'master,' also used as a word of respect after titles of names.
Sachkand	Abode of truth. This is believed to be both a physical realm and a spiritual one. The highest physical spiritual realm is Sachkand for Sikhs. If one gets to God during their life they can be living in the spirit of Sachkand. At death such a person may choose to reside at the physical Sachkand too.
Sangat	Congregation
Sarovar	Literally means 'pool of water', usually a tank of water to bathe in, which may have a boon attached to it, if one were to bathe in it.
Seva	Devotional voluntary service
Shabad	Verses of Gurbani
Shaheed	Martyr
Shaheedi	Becoming martyred

God is realised by the True Guru's Grace

Sikhi   The Sikh faith

Sri   Supreme, usually used at the start of a name to be more respectful

God is realised by the True Guru's Grace

References

1) Audio Katha, **Shaheedi Sri Guru Arjan Dev Jee**, Giani Harbhajan Singh Dudike, taken from www.gurmatveechar.com 'Sooraj Parkash Katha' folder

2) Audio Katha, **Shaheedi Sri Guru Arjan Dev Jee,** Bhai Kuljit Singh (Sikh 2 Inspire), taken from www.gurmatveechar.com 'English katha' folder

3) **Jeevan Parsang Sahib Sri Guru Arjan Dev Jee,** Bhai Vir Singh, Bhai Vir Singh Sahit Sadan, Delhi (2006)

4) **Sri Gur Partap Suraj Parkash**, Bhai Santokh Singh (1843).

5) **Twarik Guru Khalsa,** Giani Gian Singh (1891)

6) **Tuzuk-I-Jahangiri: or Memoirs of Jahangir** Translated by Alexander Rogers. Edited by Henry Beveridge. Ulan Press (2012)

7) **Fardidkoth Tika of Sri Guru Granth Sahib,** Languages Department (Bhasha Vibhag), Punjab, (1970)

8) **Sri Guru Granth Darpan,** Professor Sahib Singh – www.gurugranthdarpan.net

9) ***Guru Granth Sahib – English Version,*** (2012), Kindle ebook, www.amazon.com

10) ***Sri Guru Granth Sahib; English & Punjabi Translation,*** Manmohan Singh, SGPC, Amritsar (1962)

11) ***The Encyclopaedia of Sikhism (4 Volumes),*** Harbans Singh, Punjab University, (1995). Also available on www.thesikhencyclopaedia.com